Data Management for Libraries

Data Management for Libraries

A LITA Guide

Laura Krier
and
Carly A. Strasser

An imprint of the American Library Association

CHICAGO   2014

Printed in the United States of America

18 17 16 15 14   5 4 3 2 1

Extensive effort has gone into ensuring the reliability of the information in this book; however, the publisher makes no warranty, express or implied, with respect to the material contained herein.

ISBNs: 978-1-55570-969-3 (paper); 978-1-55570-975-4 (PDF); 978-1-55570-977-8 (ePub); 978-1-55570-976-1 (Kindle);. For more information on digital formats, visit the ALA Store at alastore.ala.org and select eEditions.

Cataloging-in-Publication data is on file with the Library of Congress.

Book design in Berkeley and Avenir. Cover image ©HunThomas/Shutterstock, Inc.

⊗ This paper meets the requirements of ANSI/NISO Z39.48-1992 (Permanence of Paper).

Contents

Preface

The buzz around data management in libraries has been growing quickly since the National Science Foundation announced that data management plans would be a required component of all grant applications starting January 2011. Many librarians felt pressed to implement data management consulting services without having a firm grasp of how best to support researchers at their institutions. In all kinds of institutions, librarians are experimenting with different service models and giving themselves crash courses in research data and the requirements for effective data management, and many are doing it with minimal guidance.

This book is intended to offer that guidance. There are a lot of elements to building an effective data management consulting service, and for many of us there are a lot of new things to learn. Jumping into a new arena, and coming up to speed as quickly as many of us have, can be challenging. Through extensive research, discussions with data management librarians around the country, and close work with data management experts, we have pulled together this planning guide to help you and your colleagues build an effective and well-used service for your researchers, faculty, and students.

Unfortunately, building a data management service is not something librarians can do on our own. Meaningful data management is a goal that should be supported at all levels of the institution, from lab assistants to department heads to the president of the university. This can be one of the biggest hurdles for libraries looking to implement these new services, but, thankfully, in recent years there has been an increasing understanding on the part of many people working in academia about the need for these kinds of services. This book offers insight into building that support in your institution and maintaining the relationships that ensure your service is successful.

Though many librarians work closely with research faculty and understand the data that is being produced, some of us are new to the world of big data. This book offers a primer on data—on why and how data should be effectively managed. We also offer some tips for talking to faculty about why data management matters, and we help you learn to conduct successful data management interviews.

This guide is here not only to help you understand data management, and how your library can be invaluable to researchers, but to help you build a service in your library. Most of the data management guidelines on the web are directed at faculty; this guide has a different approach: to help you help researchers. We walk you through every piece of a data management plan, help you make decisions about repositories and other infrastructure, and guide you through some of the difficult questions that arise about intellectual property, sharing and access, metadata, and preservation.

Data management in libraries is a new and growing area. There are sure to be changes over time as we learn more. We hope that this guide can make you and your colleagues better able to contribute to the conversation as we all work collectively to organize, preserve, and provide access to research data, as we have with other products of research.

What Is Data Management?

In nearly every field, the practice of research is changing. New technologies and tools are being used to conduct research, resulting in wholly new types of data, in vastly expanding quantities. In both the sciences and humanities, research data is increasingly taking on a digital form, living on local hard drives and remote servers, and scattered across networks. More and more, this data is born in a digital form, although physical forms of are still common within some fields of study. Some research projects combine physical and digital data, and researchers must keep track of both simultaneously. And, increasingly, research projects are producing huge sets of data that would be unmanageable without the aid of computers to process them.

These new technologies are opening the doors to greater collaboration among researchers, engineers, and computer scientists, in all fields of study. And, increasingly, librarians are being brought into these partnerships to contribute needed expertise in data management and preservation. Researchers are more interested in conducting their work than in managing and organizing the data behind it, and this is where librarians can provide valuable services and support. As librarians move into this field, it is crucial that we understand the domains in which researchers are working, and that we have a solid grasp of the kinds of research data being produced. Data types can vary widely at different institutions and in different fields of study, but whether you are at a large research library, a medical school, a liberal arts college, or in support of a particular department it is likely that research is being conducted, and that researchers need data support. You need to work closely with faculty and other researchers to know how best to support them, but a quick review of the data landscape provides a solid foundation to begin discussions.

TYPES OF RESEARCH DATA

You are likely already familiar with one major distinction between types of data: qualitative versus quantitative. Quite simply, quantitative data deals with things numerically. Qualitative data is descriptive in nature and deals with the quality of things, giving rise to categorization rather than quantification. Those in the social sciences, and in fields such as physics, are often more likely to use quantitative data, whereas fields such as anthropology and history are more likely to use qualitative data. But the truth is that the distinction between these two data types is not as hard and fast as you may believe, and people in all fields gather both types of data in their research. Beyond this basic distinction, there are many other categories of data that may be part of a research project.

Primary data is data that is collected by the researcher within a particular project. This is original data that arises from a particular experiment or observation. It is gathered and maintained by the researcher. Researchers often also use secondary data, originally created by someone else. For example, some researchers use census data gathered by a national organization to draw conclusions about a particular population. Libraries may be asked to acquire data sets for use in a particular research project, or researchers may find data sets through open-access repositories.

Both primary and secondary data take many forms. Some research projects produce observational data, which is data that has been gathered from observing a particular population or phenomenon. Experimental data, in contrast, is derived from controlled, randomized experiments. Observational data is gathered in instances where it is not possible to conduct a controlled experiment; researchers attempt to measure as many variables as possible in order to elucidate possible cause-and-effect relationships. Controlled experiments generally attempt to minimize the number of contributing factors that are not of interest in order to measure the primary variable(s) in the study.

Traditionally, observational and experimental data were both produced by human researchers, taking notes in lab notebooks. But more and more often, data is gathered with the use of computers, sensors, and other monitoring tools. These tools produce far larger data sets for researchers to collect and analyze. For example, sensors collecting traffic information can gather far more data than can a human observer, and we can gather and analyze larger sets of survey data using computers than using paper surveys filled out and reviewed by manual labor.

Research projects might also produce computational data. Computational data is the output of a computer that has taken a large set of varied data and run it through a simulation. The fields of bioinformatics and genomics are forerunners in the use of computational data. Social scientists use computational data to detect patterns and predict behaviors. Computational linguistics looks at patterns and frequency of words and phrases using n-grams. Computational data is increasingly becoming part of all fields of research.

SHARING DATA

Before the advent of large-scale, born-digital data, research data itself was not widely considered to be a valuable end product. Researchers produced papers that documented their work and drew conclusions about the data they had gathered and analyzed. The use of new technologies, though, means that some types of research data are expensive to produce. As cost rises and the size of data sets increases, data is becoming a more valuable end product. Researchers are beginning to see the advantage in sharing and reusing data sets to reach new conclusions or to better understand a related area of study. But the shift to sharing data, in addition to the final, published version of a research paper, is still in its infancy, and the move toward greater data sharing requires the support and collaboration of many members of the academic institution, including librarians.

The first steps toward an open-data landscape are being taken. Some funding bodies have instituted requirements that research papers be shared openly and that plans for managing the data produced during a research project be included in grant proposals. Many subject-specific and institution-specific data repositories are preserving and providing access to a wide range of data sets. Other repositories hold open-access copies of research papers. Although researchers sometimes remain skeptical about the value of sharing their research data, the practice is becoming more accepted. Libraries are in a unique position to provide real value to a burgeoning practice and real guidance to researchers in this new world of research.

As more funding bodies and journals issue requirements that papers and data sets be managed and shared, it is important to pay close attention to the exact specifications. For example, the National Science Foundation requires that researchers submit a brief data management plan, but they do not require that data or final papers be released in an open-access repository. The National Institutes of Health require that a data sharing plan be included for grants requesting funds over a certain amount. The National Endowment for the Humanities Office of Digital Humanities began requiring a data management plan in 2012. Some funding sources merely require that the final paper be made available in an open-access repository. Several journals, including *ISME Journal, Evolution,* and *Plant Physiology,* have open-data policies, some requiring that data be submitted to specific repositories and some merely requiring that the data be made available to those who request it.[1] The requirements can vary and are not uniformly enforced, and it is important to understand the differences between open-data requirements and open-access publication requirements and between those grants that require only that a data management plan be in place and those that require data deposit.

WHAT IS A DATA MANAGEMENT PLAN?

In many instances, a researcher is required to submit a data management plan along with the grant proposal. These plans lay out the specifics of how research data will be organized, managed, and preserved throughout the data's lifecycle, during the project and after.

The extent and amount of detail in a data management plan depend on the project itself and on the audience for which it is being created. In general, these plans require a description of the project and of the data that will be generated or used, the formats and metadata standards that will be used to store and organize data, where and how the data will be stored, in both the short and long terms, and any access provisions and legal requirements that adhere to the data. In general, funding bodies want to know that researchers have given thought to how their digital and physical data will be stored, preserved, and potentially made accessible to a wider audience.

WHAT IS DATA CURATION AND THE DATA LIFECYCLE?

There are two ways to think about the lifecycle of data: from a researcher's perspective and from an archivist's perspective. The UK Data Archive has created a "research data lifecycle" that can be useful for thinking through all the stages of data from a researcher's perspective.[2] The Digital Curation Centre has, likewise, created a "curation lifecycle model" that lays out all the processes and components involved in data curation from an archivist's or curator's perspective.[3] Both of these models are useful for libraries looking to implement data management services.

The research data lifecycle covers the lifespan of research data from creation through reuse. Most of the data services and management needs we discuss in this book are related to the research data lifecycle and to supporting the needs of researchers throughout the research process. The sequential steps of this lifecycle are creating data, processing data, analyzing data, preserving data, giving access to data, and reusing data. There are roles for librarians at most stages in this process, and each stage is made easier with good planning and management. We discuss these stages and roles for librarians in more detail in other chapters.

The data curation lifecycle model covers the lifespan of data after it has been created and analyzed and is ready to be submitted to a repository. Data curation is the management of data once it has been selected for preservation and long-term storage. This model has data and digital objects at its center and treats data curation as an iterative process. The sequential steps of the curation lifecycle are creating or receiving data, appraising and selecting data, ingesting, performing preservation actions, storing data, accessing data for use and reuse, and transforming data. There are occasional actions that may disrupt the cycle, such as reappraising and deaccessioning data sets.

Many individuals are usually involved at various stages of the data lifecycle, both during the research process and during the curation process. Where you come in will likely vary from project to project, depending on the services you elect to provide. Likewise, the data itself may be generated in different ways: some may be created, and some may be transformed from existing data sets. Some key elements must be considered at every stage of the lifecycle, including preservation planning and description. The models are intended to be used as guides for planning and are not necessarily meant to be a set of rules to follow step by step. They can be useful for framing conversations with researchers and administrators and for planning library services. We discuss all the elements of these lifecycles in more detail throughout this book.

WHAT DOES THIS HAVE TO DO WITH THE LIBRARY?

Libraries have begun stepping in to assist researchers to craft data management plans. In some instances, librarians saw a new way to contribute their skills to support researchers, and in other libraries external pressure brought librarians to the table. In any case, librarians have a great opportunity to expand our services in ways that can benefit faculty, build stronger relationships between libraries and research communities, and continue to play a role in the preservation of scholarly communication.

This last is the real key to our role in data management. Libraries have long been crucial players in the scholarly communication chain. We have been responsible for preserving and making accessible the scholarly record. Now, the form that the scholarly record takes is changing, and we must make sure that we are ready and able to continue our role in preserving and providing access. We can help researchers adapt to these changes by taking on new roles in the shifting infrastructure of scholarly communication.

WHAT'S IN IT FOR FACULTY?

Data sharing is not a universal given in the scientific community yet, but nearly all researchers can see the benefit of improved data management. Jahnke and colleagues, in their Council in Library and Information Resources report *The Problem of Data*, note that researchers "understand that poor data management can be costly to their research and that access to greater technical expertise, through either a consultant or additional training, would be useful for their work."[4] Few researchers are happy with their own data management practices. They comment that they do not have time for the organizational and administrative work that goes into carefully managing and documenting data, and that they never received explicit training in data management practices. Additionally, many researchers work in fields that lack widely used and well-documented metadata standards or a common integrated data infrastructure.[5]

It can be challenging to convince faculty to take the time to plan for data management at the outset of a research project. The key to working successfully with faculty in this area is to show them how they can benefit from planning and organizing their work ahead of time, then maintaining their data accurately during their project. They will be more interested in working with you to create an effective data management plan if they can understand how it will help them to complete and publish their work.

One oft-cited data management problem for principle investigators is related to work done by their research assistants and graduate students. In many labs, research assistants are responsible for managing their own data. However, the varied data management practices that result from this ad hoc lab practice can create a lack of continuity and lead to missing or incomprehensible data when a particular research assistant leaves the project.[6] Data is easier to retrieve and use, whoever produced it, when it is managed properly.

Additionally, some researchers have discussed the difficulty of going back to their own previous data sets for reuse or reexamination when the original work suffered poor data management practices. Without good documentation and contextual information, it can be difficult to understand how and why data was captured in the first place.

Good data management reduces the amount of work required in interpreting and compiling information at the end of a research project. When good documentation is created while research is ongoing, it does not need to be reconstructed at a later date. Managing data consistently throughout a project can lead to greater confidence in the accuracy of that data and greater efficiency in analyzing it and producing a paper.

You encounter a range of attitudes, beliefs, needs, and understandings toward research and research data as you begin to work with faculty. Working in this area makes use of many of your skills, including conducting a data interview that helps you assess what a researcher really needs, understanding how to organize a variety of data types, and helping researchers make the right decisions about access and preservation for their particular data. Librarians are well suited to move into this area, even though some of it may be new to us. Throughout the process of establishing a data management service, you are—first and foremost—doing what librarians do best: establishing relationships on your campus and discovering the best ways to be of service to your unique constituents.

NOTES

1. See the Open Access Directory's list of open-data policies for a growing list of these journals at http://oad.simmons.edu/oadwiki/Journal_open-data_policies.

2. "Research Data Lifecycle," UK Data Archive, http://data-archive.ac.uk/create-manage/life-cycle.

3. "DCC Curation Lifecycle Model," Digital Curation Centre, www.dcc.ac.uk/resources/curation-lifecycle-model.

4. Lori Jahnke, Andrew Asher, and Spencer D. C. Keralis, *The Problem of Data* (Washington, DC: Council on Library and Information Resources, August 2012), 15.

5. Dharma Akmon, Ann Zimmerman, Morgan Daniels, and Margaret Hedstrom, "The Application of Archival Concepts to a Data-Intensive Environment: Working with Scientists to Understand Data Management and Preservation Needs," *Archival Science* 11, no. 3/4 (November 2011): 329–348.

6. Ibid.

Starting a New Service

S tarting a new data management service is much like starting any new service; you need staff who are willing to take on new roles and responsibilities, you need to identify the members of your community who could benefit from the service, and you need to be sure that what you are offering meets the needs of your users. The struggle for resources in libraries is a well-known issue, so investing time, energy, and money into something new must be done thoughtfully and with a good balance of caution and initiative.

People often talk about the benefits of being willing to fail, and they are right. Having the willingness to make mistakes is important when you are trying new things. But you cannot simply fail. You must also be willing to make adjustments based on what you learn from those mistakes. If you begin offering data management services with the idea that you are working on a pilot project, or are in a beta phase, you can ensure that all participants are working with the mindset that you will be correcting course as you go, changing practices based on what works and what doesn't for your users and your staff.

Embark on building a suite of data management services with the understanding that you will all be learning as you go—not just your staff but users as well. Be willing to admit when you don't know something, and willing to find the information you don't already have. Think of the process of developing a new service as an iterative one: if at first you don't succeed, make small changes and try again. You also don't need to try to do everything at once. Talk honestly about your resources to determine on what level you are able to offer assistance and knowledge to your community.

Most important, don't try to build your data management services in a vacuum. Active engagement of all stakeholders makes the difference between a useful service and a languishing service that people forget is even offered.

COLLABORATING

There are a wide variety of data management services that you might provide to researchers. When deciding on the scope of services you want to offer, it is important to think honestly about your strengths and about the ability of your staff to take on new tasks, or of your library to hire dedicated librarians to run a data management service.

For some libraries, the impetus to begin offering data management services is coming from outside of the library—either from researchers themselves, asking for help, or from administrators who want to engage in stronger data curation practices at the institution. If you do not already have engagement and support from administration and department heads, this is an important first step in providing meaningful services to your constituents. Like all library services, data services are more effective if you have institutional buy-in before you begin to offer them. Not only does this ensure support, but you have a much better shot at offering the right services if you work with researchers, administrators, grant management offices, and other campus constituents to craft them. This also serves to market your services and get the word out to your users.

To determine where your efforts would best be spent, it is important to engage with researchers at your institution. Working with researchers to identify the assistance and tools they need is more productive than building services based on assumptions or the services other libraries are providing.[1] One excellent strategy for building data management services is to identify enthusiastic researchers willing to work with you as pilot participants. Using a single research project to pilot a new service can help you identify strengths and weaknesses and learn what works well and what strategies need further development and consideration.

Working with researchers can also help you identify what services are actually needed. If most of the researchers in your institution have already identified subject repositories where they prefer to deposit their data, implementing an institutional repository might be a waste of effort for library staff. But if your administration wants to collect and preserve the breadth of the institution's research, or institutional records, an institutional repository might be the cornerstone of your services.

Be sure to consider carefully the services you are interested in offering in light of the needs of your institution and the interests of your stakeholders.

Building institutional support from the ground up, by starting with researchers, is often a smart tactic. If faculty request data management services, administrators are often more likely to listen. Talk to researchers about what they need and how you may be able to help, and enlist them as allies. This may give you the leverage you need to make hiring decisions or request funding for service projects. Building consensus around a particular need is much more fruitful than waging that battle for money or resources by yourself.

Another consideration, suggested by Lage and colleagues, is to offer different levels of service to meet different needs, from backups and archiving to full-service metadata assistance.[2] You and your staff may want to lay out a set of services that range from least involved to most involved, then make determinations along that scale of what you are willing and capable of offering.

It may also be worth while to reach out to other institutions and government bodies to discuss ways that you can collaborate to offer more extensive services. For example, a team of librarians at the University of Guelph recognized a need in the field of agri-environmental sciences for a subject repository. They collaborated with the Ontario Ministry of Agriculture, Food, and Rural Affairs, and the Dataverse Network project to build a subject repository available to researchers in the field.[3] There could be similar opportunities for your library to create services that reach beyond the bounds of your particular institution.

DATA LIFECYCLE

As we mention in chapter 1, thinking about the data lifecycle can be a useful tool for beginning to sketch out the types of data services you might want to offer. Each stage of the lifecycle requires different services, and this model can be a helpful way to think about what you can and want to do.

The first stage of the lifecycle is data creation. Before data creation begins, researchers should think about finding an effective way to save and store data during the gathering process, settling on a useful metadata strategy and ensuring that all research participants understand and can use the metadata schema, ensuring that all participants have access to the data and data-gathering tools, ensuring that all privacy and confidentiality issues have been considered and managed, and crafting a data management plan. There are a variety of ways the library can be involved at this stage, from offering sample data management plans, to working closely throughout the research planning process to craft a metadata strategy, to offering servers for storing digital data, to creating customized data management software for a particular research project. You might help create organizing strategies for files and documentation.[4] You might provide metadata training services for lab assistants or work with campus IT to offer storage solutions for data during the research process. The level of service you are able to offer during the data creation process depends on your staffing capabilities and resources. Reach out to other departments on campus to find out what tools and services they can offer, and consider partnering with them to offer more efficient or more robust services. Is there networked file or data storage available through campus IT? What services do grant support offices already offer, and can you collaborate with them?

After data has been created or gathered, researchers begin processing it. This involves transcribing, digitizing, validating and cleaning, anonymizing, and storing. This is the stage where all the planning is put to use. If a researcher has decided ahead of time on effective storage, metadata, and workflows, the data processing stage will move more smoothly. You might offer storage solutions or tools that help researchers create metadata as research is being processed. You might even help researchers create descriptive metadata during the research process.

During the analysis phase, researchers are doing most of the real meat of their work—interpreting their data and producing their research outputs. Librarians do not often have a strong role at this stage, but any services provided at earlier stages make this part of their work much easier.

Preserving data, the next stage, involves migrating data to suitable formats and media for preservation, creating backups, and creating any additional metadata that is necessary for preservation. Librarians can offer real help in this stage, for many researchers do not know what is required for effective data preservation. You might simply provide information about best practices for preservation formats, or you might perform the actual data migration. You might decide to give workshops or trainings that inform researchers about what is involved in preservation or offer a complete suite of preservation services. There is a wide range of help you can provide for researchers who want to preserve their data sets.

Giving access to data is also an area where librarians can provide valuable services. You might decide to host a local repository, but even if you don't you will want to work with researchers to ensure that they are meeting all funder requirements for data retention and accessibility. You might be able to help them identify a suitable repository or walk them through the process of submission. You might be able to help them organize and format their data for deposit or craft the necessary metadata for submission. Whatever repository is being used, the researcher needs to provide information about how the data will be used and by whom, access requirements and restrictions, and information to allow the repository to assess the scholarly quality of the data. Additionally, you might be able to increase the discoverability of data sets by cataloging them in various discovery systems or readying them for harvesting into open archives of data sets.

If your library has decided to host a data repository, the data curation lifecycle is important for you to understand. The data curation lifecycle involves decisions from accessioning data through preservation and migration to ongoing provision of access and retention decisions.

The implementation of a data repository is a big project, and you may decide that it will not be part of your data management services. If you do decide to implement a repository, you probably want to do further research on that process and the technology and staff requirements involved. See appendix A for a list of resources that can assist you in the process of establishing an institutional repository.

TRAINING AND INSTRUCTION

Researchers may have been trained in their field and become active in the process of conducting research without receiving any training in managing research data.[5] Many people are beginning to talk about offering basic training on data management and data literacy as part of the library's instructional program. These courses could be offered to graduate students or to lab assistants who are beginning work on a new project. They might be offered to undergraduates as well, depending on the institution's curriculum and the students' level of involvement in the research. Faculty can help you target training to the right audiences if you are unsure.

Data management workshops can be conducted as one-off workshops or designed to be integrated with a research project from the start. The options you offer depend on the needs of research teams at your institution. You might want to work closely with a particular research team to train them to create the metadata necessary for their research, or you might offer more general workshops on the basic principles of data management.

If you choose to offer data training, it is wise to work with your instruction department. They have lots of insight into the types of trainings that work best at your institution and can offer advice about establishing relationships with faculty and working with them to craft effective instruction. You might want to gather a focus group of researchers from different departments to review your proposed instructional tools and plans.

STAFFING

You may have already designated a staff person as the data management librarian. You may even be the librarian who has been thus designated. But it is unlikely that one person alone can run a successful data management service. The wide range of activities involved in data management can draw on the skills and strengths of many different people in your library. For example, reference or liaison librarians are typically best suited for conducting data interviews but not the strongest candidates for building a data repository or migrating data into a preservation-friendly format.

If you are lucky, you can hire staff dedicated to data services. But even a dedicated data librarian cannot do it alone. This librarian must work closely with rest of the staff to draw on their existing knowledge of faculty and other partners in the campus community. There are some specific skills a data librarian should have, and you may be wondering what qualities and experiences you should look for when hiring one. Some areas of expertise a data librarian should have are knowledge in the areas of copyright, intellectual property, licensing, and research privacy; project management skills; a background in or familiarity with the open-access movement; metadata skills; and experience using data analysis tools. You may also want someone with instructional experience or with experience working with faculty and researchers. The Australian National Data Service has published some generic data librarian job descriptions, which are included here in appendix B.

Most likely, though, in our era of constant downsizing, data services are being added to the already heavy workloads of existing staff. How do you build enthusiasm for these new roles when many librarians already feel stretched too thin? Integrating data services into the strategic plan and vision of your library, and involving librarians in the process of crafting that strategic plan, can go a long way. It can help to build awareness of data services as another component of the work librarians have long done in the scholarly communication arena. Carpenter and colleagues discuss the ways that new roles for librarians in data management are complementary to their traditional roles in the scholarly communication process:

organizing and providing access, helping scholars find sources, and preserving the written work of the scholarly community.[6]

If you are adding to existing roles, consider your staff closely. Think about their strengths and weaknesses before delegating various aspects of data services. Find out what motivates your staff; this can help you to engage them in the process of building new services. There are a number of resources you can find to help you learn to motivate and engage staff in institutional change. Change is more comfortable for everyone when they are included in the direction, rationale, and pace of that change. Include your staff in decision making about what kinds of new roles they might take on. Do you have liaison librarians? They are naturals for introducing data services to their departments, for conducting data interviews, and for finding the right participants for pilot projects. Your liaison librarians can be the public face of your data services, building support and recognition around campus.

If you do not have a solid liaison program, reference and instruction librarians are also well positioned to take on these roles. They have likely already established relationships with faculty and with the research departments on campus. But don't limit your thoughts about outreach to those who normally serve in a public services role. An acquisitions librarian who has developed close relationships with faculty and researchers may be well suited to reach out to those people to talk about data. Find out which of your librarians have relationships on campus, not only with researchers but with IT, grants offices, and other key players who can partner with you to build effective services.

Some argue that, to provide really effective data services, liaison librarians need a solid grounding in the domains with which they are working. If you do not have the resources to dedicate to acquiring specific domain knowledge, you may want to focus on training researchers in data management and curation skills rather than embedding librarians into research projects and research departments. The level of involvement you can and should provide depends on the knowledge, ability, and interest of your staff and the kinds of resources you have available, as well as the level of interest of researchers.

You might elect one person to lead the data services team, but that person should not be expected to run a successful data service alone. The best way to ensure the successful introduction of data services is to engage the whole library staff or build a team of key players who can take on different roles. Create a data management team with some librarians who are good at outreach, some who excel at metadata management, and some who are technically adept at working with new

15

software and systems. This puts you in a position to address most of the data needs of your researchers with a well-rounded team. Data librarians need to work with research data, metadata, and technology as well as with a range of stakeholders. They have to craft policy, work closely with faculty, understand digital preservation, and possibly even take on data acquisitions and licensing roles. Your library is best served when you can bring together a team that demonstrates all of these strength and empower them to learn together and from one another. Engaged, enthusiastic staff give any new service a greater chance of success.

NOTES

1. Lori Jahnke, Andrew Asher, and Spencer D. C. Keralis, *The Problem of Data* (Washington, DC: Council on Library and Information Resources, August 2012).

2. Kathryn Lage, Barbara Losoff, and Jack Maness, "Receptivity to Library Involvement in Scientific Data Curation: A Case Study at the University of Colorado Boulder," *Portal: Libraries and the Academy* 11 (2011): 915–937.

3. Wayne Johnston, "The Alchemist's Guide to Research Data: Ensuring Data Usability," presented at the LITA National Forum, Columbus, OH, October 2012.

4. Tracy Gabridge, "The Last Mile: Liaison Roles in Curating Science and Engineering Research Data," *Research Library Issues,* no. 265 (2009): 15–21.

5. Dharma Akmon, Ann Zimmerman, Morgan Daniels, and Margaret Hedstrom, "The Application of Archival Concepts to a Data-Intensive Environment: Working with Scientists to Understand Data Management and Preservation Needs," *Archival Science* 11, no. 3/4 (November 2011): 329–348. doi:10.1007/s10502-011-9151-4.

6. Maria Carpenter, Jolie Graybill, Jared Offord, and Mary Piorun, "Envisioning the Library's Role in Scholarly Communication in the Year 2025," *Portal: Libraries and the Academy* 11, no. 2 (April 2011): 659–681. doi:10.1353/pla.2011.0014.

Data Management Plans: An Overview

Data management plans have become a frequent topic of discussion recently among many librarians, researchers, funders, and administrators. You have undoubtedly had conversations about data management plans within your own library. Although these plans have been around for as long as data has been collected, they have become more nuanced and complex along with the rise of digital data. Increasing attention to data management plans can be most readily attributed to their requirement by funders.[1] The organizations and institutions that pay for data collection are concerned about the availability of that data well into the future. They want a high return on their investment.

There are stakeholder groups besides funders that are concerned about data management, access, and preservation; however, they recognize the critical role that funders play in mandating data management plans. An interagency working group on digital data recommended that funders promote and enforce the creation of such plans, stating that "advance planning for data preservation and access can ensure that appropriate, cost-effective strategies are identified, and the digital products of research can be made widely available to catalyze progress."[2]

DO RESEARCHERS NEED HELP WITH DATA MANAGEMENT PLANS?

In one word, yes. Steinhart and colleagues have shown that primary investigators at Cornell University were not prepared or knowledgeable enough to meet new requirements by the National Science Foundation for data management plans.[3] In general, researchers were not sure whether they were following standards for data collection and organization, most were not creating metadata (and those who did were not following standards), and they were not knowledgeable about intellectual property and data governance issues. Overall, there were major uncertainties about what the new requirements for data management plans mean and how they would meet these requirements.

Peters and Dryden conducted a similar survey at the University of Houston.[4] They assessed current data management practices on campus via interviews with scientists leading research groups. Their main findings were that researchers need help finding data management requirements, writing those data management plans for their grant proposals, and finding data-related services on campus.

THE ROLE OF INFORMATION PROFESSIONALS

In reality, the skill set required for helping researchers with data management is readily available in academic libraries.[5] Librarians and information specialists have a unique role in the data management arena. Gathering, organizing, and preserving information have been the charge of librarians for centuries; articulating data management plans is simply a modern manifestation of this charge. Accepting the responsibility of educating and assisting researchers in their preparation of such plans requires basic knowledge about plan components as well as an intricate knowledge of the particular facets of the researcher's field, project, and data sets. Obtaining this knowledge requires interviews and research (see chapter 4).

There are an array of roles librarians can take on in working with faculty to craft data management plans. Many libraries dedicate a portion of their website to data management plans, offering a basic outline and guidelines or sample plans. Many of these sites have become well known in the library community for their straightforward advice and thoroughness, including the Massachusetts Institute of Technology Library's "Data Management and Publishing Guide" and the data management guides and tools published by the California Digital Library.[6] You may want to publish information that is specially tailored for researchers at your institution; for example, if you have a department working on digital humanities, you will want to provide information about the grant requirements for the National Endowment for the Humanities.

Another way to address multiple researchers at once is to offer workshops on crafting data management plans. These can also be targeted for particular types of grant requirements or particular types of research. Workshops can offer a generalized picture of data management or offer more specific help for those who have to write plans for upcoming grants. The types of workshops you offer should be guided by the interests of your faculty.

Some librarians offer one-on-one consultations with researchers who are faced with writing data management plans. These can be quite useful and usually begin with a data management interview. There are often issues of preservation and documentation that researchers have never considered; by conducting a thorough interview, a knowledgeable data librarian can fill in the gaps researchers might not even realize exist.

Your institution, your available resources, and the needs of your faculty guide you to determine the scope of data management services you want to offer, but an understanding of the common components of a data management plan, and why they are useful for researchers, is an excellent foundation for whatever services you choose to offer.

MOTIVATING THE RESEARCHER
TO CREATE A DATA MANAGEMENT PLAN

Funder requirements for data management plans are forcing researchers to create plans but are not requiring that those plans be of high quality or particularly extensive. For example, the NSF requires a two-page plan to accompany a fifteen-page research proposal;[7] it is highly unlikely that a well-formed and thorough data management plan can be described in two pages. For researchers to create high-quality plans, they must be informed of the benefits of investing time and energy in those plans. Data management is time consuming, potentially expensive, and currently poorly incentivized. You may use the following points to motivate the researcher to create a high-quality plan:

> *Data management plans save time for the researcher over the long term.* Effort spent before data collection begins can be focused on the wider context of the project rather than the details of a specific task or item. This ensures that the decisions made about data organization,

management, and preservation are beneficial to long-term goals. Less time is spent rearranging, renaming, searching for, or otherwise handling files and data sets if their organization and management are thought out well in advance.[8]

Plans prevent upheaval brought about by staffing changes. Often data and projects are shared among researchers within a given laboratory or research group. If consistent, up-to-date data management plans are in place, the fact that staff come and go has no effect on the accessibility or usability of that data. The knowledge about data management, organization, and archiving stays within the group.[9]

Plans help with data queries. Most researchers at some time or another have been asked to provide or share their data. This may be in the context of verifying results, sharing data with a student or colleague, or contributing data to a separate project. If solid, well-constructed data management plans are readily available to accompany the data, there is no need to provide further explanation and spend time or energy preparing the data for sharing.[10]

Plans link personnel roles, responsibilities, activity, and support over the life of a project. If plans are considered integral to the project itself, then all personnel affiliated with the project are aware of the plan's existence and adhere to it. Roles and responsibilities are clearly defined, and any management or organizational changes are documented in the manner outlined by the plan. Creating the plan is not a separate or burdensome task but an important part of establishing how to handle the project's data.

GENERAL ADVICE ABOUT DATA MANAGEMENT PLANS

Although researchers are likely aware of the new data management plans requirements they are obliged to meet, they are not likely to be knowledgeable about where to begin, how to start, or who to ask for help. Jones offers some basic advice to researchers on how to plan for data management.[11] You should be aware of this advice when consulting with researchers about their data:

Researchers should consult and collaborate with experts in the fields relevant to data management. These include technical experts and IT staff at their institutions, legal advisors, ethics boards, and potential repositories for data. To best point researchers to the resources they need as they develop data management services, consider developing relationships with these institutional experts.

Use existing intellectual and infrastructure resources. Researchers should work closely with you, and with other information professionals, and take advantage of department servers, campus-licensed software, and other technological resources. In general, be aware of the technological and intellectual resources available on campus to meet data management needs.

Justify data management decisions. Researchers must ensure that discipline and institutional standards are being followed and that all decisions are defensible based on those standards or the specific needs of the project. Librarians can help researchers learn about standards and best practices in their fields.

Be prepared to implement the plan. All required software, hardware, and personnel required to carry out the data management plan should be ready if the grant is funded.

Other important points to emphasize:

Data management plans are an integral part of grant applications and should not be considered an afterthought. Engage with researchers before they come to you to help them see how data management plans can benefit them, even if they are not required for a particular grant or project.

Plans are living documents. They should and will change over the course of a project. Long-term preservation, access, and interoperability require management of the full data lifecycle.[12]

Plans are enhanced through collaboration. Librarians, IT professionals, researchers, repository personnel, and data managers all have unique experience and expertise to lend to the creation of a data management plan.

THE MAIN COMPONENTS
OF A DATA MANAGEMENT PLAN

Although data management plans can take many forms, several main components must be addressed in all plans: (1) description of data and metadata; (2) discussion of security, ethics, and intellectual property; (3) plans for data access, sharing, and reuse; (4) plans for short-term management and storage; (5) plans for long-term management, storage, and preservation; and (6) any resources that are needed or available. It is important to consult with the specific funder's requirements when preparing plans, since these components may be combined, split apart, or further defined.[13]

Data and Metadata Description

The description of a project's data and metadata is likely to be the largest section of any data management plant. Plan creators must consider the following questions:

Basic information about the data being collected or produced (i.e., brief, general, and nontechnical)

- What types of data will be produced (e.g., experimental, observational, raw or derived, physical collections, models, simulations, curriculum materials, software)?
- How will the data be acquired?
- When and where will the data be acquired?
- How much data will be acquired?
- How will data be processed?

Information about existing data

- Will any existing data be used? Include information about its origins.
- What is the relationship between existing data and data to be collected?

Information about files, formats, and directories that will be used during data collection, including file naming conventions, software that will be used to gather data, and file formats

Information about quality assurance and quality control measures

- What will be done during sample collection?

- What will be done during analysis?
- What will be done during data processing?

Information about project personnel

- Who will be responsible for data management *during* the project, and what does that entail?
- Who will be responsible for data management *after* the project, and what does that entail?

Metadata considerations

- What contextual details are needed to make the data meaningful?
- How will this metadata be created or captured?
- When and by whom will the metadata be created or captured?
- What form will the metadata take (standards) and why?

Security, Ethics, and Intellectual Property

Data security entails ensuring that the data is safe throughout the life of the project and that only those who should have access to the data are able to access it. Data ethics are important in cases where there may be sensitive data. Sensitive data includes personally identifiable information, data on protected or endangered species, and data involving native human populations. Intellectual property concerns fall under data governance; there is much confusion and debate surrounding data governance issues, especially given that digital data and technology are evolving rapidly and misuse of intellectual property is common. One example of a complicating factor related to intellectual property is that data cannot be copyrighted since it is essentially a collection of facts; arrangements of data can, however, be copyrighted. It is important to consult with ethics boards and legal advisors at the institutional level to ensure that all data governance issues are being addressed properly. Chapter 8 on data governance gives some insight into intellectual property issues.

Security

- Are there ethical/legal obligations for privacy and protection?
- How will data be managed to protect this privacy?
- How will the data be stored, paying special attention to security measures?
- Who will have access to the data, and at what stage of the project?

Ethics

- Are there ethical and privacy issues that may prohibit sharing some or all of the data sets?
- If these issues exist, how will they be resolved?

Intellectual property

- Who owns rights to the data created?
- Will the data set(s) be covered by copyright?
- If the data set(s) will be covered by copyright, who owns the copyright?
- How will the data set(s) be licensed?
- If any existing data sets are used, what are their licensing restrictions?

Data Access, Sharing, and Reuse

Many of the existing funding requirements for data management plans are focused on access to data.[14] Although data sharing is strongly encouraged across funders, publishers, and institutions, it is not a common practice in most disciplines. Requiring that researchers describe their plans for allowing others to access their data, and assessing whether those plans were followed, is a strong motivator for researchers to share their data. Anticipating and planning for data reuse encourage good data management practices throughout the life of the project.

Here are some questions for the researcher to consider with regard to data sharing:

- Which data will be shared?
- At what stage will the data be shared (raw, processed, reduced, analyzed)?
- Will you need written consent from any participants to share or reuse the data beyond the project?
- Are there obligations from funders, institutions, or journal publishers to share all or part of the data?
- When will the data be made available?
- Who will be able to access the data when it is made available?
- What is the process for gaining access to the data?
- Where will the data be shared? (share-upon-request; self-created archives, such as a website; published as supplemental material; published in a repository)[15]

- Will there be restrictions on access to the data? What restrictions and for how long? What is the rationale for these restrictions? Does the original data collector/creator/principle investigator retain the right to use the data before opening it up to wider use? Are there any embargo periods for political, commercial, or patent reasons?

Data citation and proper crediting are also important considerations. Researchers want to be assured that they will receive proper credit for data sets they share:

- How should their data be cited when used by others?
- How will they address the issue of persistent identification for citation?

Short-Term Storage and Management

Any data management plan should consider both long-term and short-term management and storage of data; the concerns and issues are different for these two time frames. Short-term management considerations include concerns about securing data during the course of the research project and while subsequent work with the data sets is ongoing. Researchers should consider the following:

- How will version control be handled?
- How will data be backed up and secured on a daily, weekly, and monthly basis?
- Who will have access to the data? What permissions will those personnel have (read and/or write)?
- Which data need to be stored in the short term, and in what formats?
- What institutional support may be used (e.g., IT resources, repositories, servers)?
- How will collaborators gain access to the data?
- How will remote access be gained?
- Will data be available offline or online, and to whom?

Long-Term Storage, Management, and Preservation

Data management plans should clarify what approach the researcher plans to take to ensure data is available for use and reuse in the future. This includes long-term storage of the data in a repository, plans for ongoing management of the data (e.g., updating metadata or contact information for the researcher who collected the data), and preservation tasks (e.g., ensuring file formats are up-to-date).

What data will be preserved for the long-term? It is not always necessary for all data to be archived. Some preliminary and intermediate data may not be useful and the costs associated with preserving that data not justified. If it is not clear from the start which data set components should be kept, how will this be decided during the course of the project? In general, data with long-term value should be selected for long-term management. Long-term value is nebulous and difficult to predict; however, the researcher most familiar with the data being collected is likely able to make this judgment call.

Instruct researchers to safeguard all data "behind the graph." In other words, any data used to generate results presented in publications or other public-facing materials should be maintained. The following questions should be asked about any data determined to be worth long-term preservation:

- For how long will the data be preserved?
- Where will the data be preserved? What repository will be used, and what are the retention policies?
- What data transformations need to occur to prepare the data for preservation?
- What metadata/documentation will be submitted alongside the data sets to make the data reusable?
- Who will be responsible for preparing data for long-term storage during the project?
- Who will be the main contact person for the archived data?
- How will responsibility for the data be transferred, if needed?
- How will ongoing costs be paid?
- Who will be responsible for ensuring that data is linked via persistent identifiers to the project and to any relevant publications?

Resources

One of the biggest pitfalls of implementing a high-quality data management plan is a lack of necessary resources. Good data stewardship is by no means free; there are many costs associated with hardware, software, personnel, and the like. Funders encourage grant applicants to include these costs in the budget of the grant. Consider the following:

Personnel

- Are there sufficient resources and expertise in the research team to manage, preserve, and share the data effectively?
- Is additional specialist expertise (or training for existing staff) required? If so, where will this be found? From a library perspective, if you are planning to offer data consulting services, will you offer them at no charge to researchers? Where will your resources come from?

Infrastructure

- What hardware and software are needed to implement the data management plan? Is it readily available?
- Is there existing infrastructure available for use? If so, is it sufficient to manage, store, and analyze the data generated by the research? If not, where and when will this hardware and software be acquired? Does the library want to acquire licenses to data management software and tools for use by faculty and students?

Appendix C offers examples of data management plans written for the NSF.

FUNDER REQUIREMENTS

Although the basic components of a data management plan are similar across funders, there are significant differences in the structure, length, and detail required. It is important to note that plan guidelines for all funders are likely to change often. Finding the most up-to-date information is critical for ensuring that plans satisfy all requirements.

Dietrich and colleagues surveyed the data management plan guidelines of ten funders to clarify the requirements researchers face and how librarians can help via service offerings.[16] They identified seventeen critical elements that guidelines could address; no single policy addressed all seventeen of these elements, and most policies were missing many of the critical elements. They concluded that there are gaps between the goals that funders have in mind for data management and their assistance in implementation; it is within this gap that you and your library can offer services to assist researchers.

A Special Note about National Science Foundation Requirements

In January 2011, the NSF began requiring that a two-page data management plan accompany all proposals. The NSF grant proposal guidelines provide higher-level guidance for these plans, outlining five basic sections that are similar to those outlined in this chapter.[17] It is important to note, however, that some divisions and directorates within the NSF have more extensive or detailed requirements that applicants must follow in addition to the general across-NSF guidelines. Furthermore, some specific funding opportunities within a division may have more rigorous requirements for their data management plans. These should be the applicant's top priority when creating a plan.[18]

NOTES

1. D. Dietrich, T. Adamus, A. Miner, and G. Steinhart, "De-mystifying the Data Management Requirements of Research Funders," *Issues in Science and Technology Librarianship,* Summer 2012. doi:10.5062/F44M92G2.

2. Interagency Working Group on Digital Data, *Harnessing the Power of Digital Data for Science and Society* (Washington, DC: Committee on Science of the National Science and Technology Council, 2009), 23.

3. G. Steinhart, E. Chen, F. Arguillas, D. Dietrich, and S. Kramer, "Prepared to Plan? A Snapshot of Researcher Readiness to Address Data Management Planning Requirements," *Journal of eScience Librarianship* 1, no. 2 (2012): Article 1.

4. C. Peters and A. R. Dryden, "Assessing the Academic Library's Role in Campus-Wide Research Data Management: A First Step at the University of Houston," *Science and Technology Libraries* 30 (2011): 387–403.

5. P. Hswe and A. Holt, "Joining in the Enterprise of Response in the Wake of the NSF Data Management Planning Requirement," *Research Library Issues,* no. 274 (February 2011):11–17.

6. Massachusetts Institute of Technology Library, "Manage Your Data," https://libraries .mit.edu/guides/subjects/data-management/index.html; California Digital Library, "Manage Your Data," www.cdlib.org/services/uc3/datamanagement/.

7. "Scientists Seeking NSF Funding Will Soon Be Required to Submit Data Management Plans" (Press Release 10-077, May 10, 2010.), National Science Foundation, www.nsf.gov/news/news_summ.jsp?cntn_id=116928.

8. S. Jones, *How to Develop a Data Management and Sharing Plan.* DCC How-to Guides. (Edinburgh: Digital Curation Centre, 2011).

9. University of Southampton, "Research Data Management: An Introduction," 2012. www.soton.ac.uk/library/research/researchdata/research_data_introduction.html.

10. Jones, *How to Develop.*

11. Ibid.

12. Interagency Working Group on Digital Data, *Harnessing the Power.*

13. Dietrich et al., *De-mystifying.*

14. University of Southampton, "Research Data Management."

15. T. Vision, B. Hayes, and R. Merinshaw, "Data Management Have You Down in the DMPs? How to Approach Your First NSF Data Management Plan." https://docs.google.com/document/pub?id=1JuGwQ93uAAlGYy_KOXB7UzKttooIvHK46cUp0AzooCo.

16. Dietrich et al., *De-mystifying.*

17. National Science Foundation, Grant Proposal Guide, January 2013, www.nsf.gov/pubs/policydocs/pappguide/nsf13001/gpg_2.jsp#dmp.

18. U.C. Berkeley Science Libraries, Preparing Data Management Plans for NSF Grant Applications," 2011. available at http://www.lib.berkeley.edu/CHEM/data/nsf/nsf_dmp.pdf.

29

The Data Management Interview

Most of your work in providing data services to researchers at your institution centers on the data interview. Data interviews have a lot in common with reference interviews, so it is likely that members of your team already have skills that can suit your library well in this arena. In a data interview, it is not only about capturing what the researcher is saying, but also about asking the right questions in order to get at the things the researcher is not saying that are nevertheless important for effective data management. Researchers at Purdue University point out in their study that librarians use many of the same skills in data management interviews as in reference interviews: the ability to negotiate; to advocate for, promote, and market services; and to manage users' expectations and gracefully handle complaints.[1] And, in the end, a data interview is about connecting the researcher to the resources that help them conduct their work efficiently and effectively.

In the same way that reference librarians need a solid understanding of the resources available before providing reference services, data librarians need a good understanding of the types of research being conducted at their institutions, the types of resources available from different departments on campus, and the accepted practices in the wider fields that will be supported. You should understand this information at least cursorily before ever conducting the first data interview. It sounds like a lot to know, but the good news is that you don't have to be an expert. In many cases, you learn more as you work with researchers on campus. The most important skills are knowing when to ask questions and where to find the answers.

Librarians use many skills in reference interviews that can be helpful in data interviews. Restate what a researcher says to clarify your understanding, and ask open questions. Ask questions in different ways to elicit fuller answers. Allow researchers to talk without interruption, and summarize what they say before moving on. Do not offer advice or guidance until you have a full understanding of where the researchers are coming from and what kind of data they will be working with. Being a good, close listener goes a long way when working with researchers.

Building relationships with other service providers on campus is key in providing good data services. If the IT department provides file servers and backup servers for faculty and student use, or if the physics department endorses a particular subject-specific repository, these are things you should know about. Additionally, learning about the types of research done on your campus helps you know to whom you should reach out and where your services might be most useful. Knowing about the common practices in those fields helps you make useful suggestions and point to the right resources.

One good place to start thinking about how to work with researchers on your campus is by using a data curation profile. Researchers at Purdue University Libraries and the Graduate School of Library and Information Science at the University of Illinois began thinking about how to reach out to researchers. They wanted to address the fact that librarians do not always have a solid understanding of data practices in various research fields. Through interviews with science and engineering faculty, they constructed a set of data curation profiles, which describe how researchers currently create and administer data and what they would like to do with data that they are not currently doing. This team then put together a workshop and a toolkit to help librarians understand what they need to know before conducting a data interview.[2]

The Data Curation Profiles Toolkit (http://datacurationprofiles.org) includes a worksheet for faculty and an interview manual and specific script that can guide librarians. The authors of the manual did a wonderful job in writing questions in a straightforward and easy-to-understand way, avoiding jargon that might be understood differently by researchers and librarians. The questions allow librarian and researcher to discuss the lifecycle of the data and how it will be analyzed and used, how the data is shared during the project, and how access should be provided both during and after the research. The worksheet, too, can be useful for allowing a researcher to lay out all the concerns related to the data and see it all in one place.

A similar research project was conducted at the University of Colorado–Boulder. Lage, Losoff, and Maness conducted extensive interviews with researchers and

developed eight personas representing an aggregation of the faculty and graduate student researchers they interviewed.[3] These personas reveal that the needs,
community practices, and understandings of research and data vary widely across
different research fields. And though every institution, department, and researcher
exhibits unique qualities, these eight personas can be useful to help you begin to
understand the issues that arise when working with researchers in your institution.

The eight personas crafted by the team at the University of Colorado range in
their level of interest, the amount of support they feel they already have, the data
storage issues they face, and the amount of privacy their data requires. One thing
the team noted is that there is not always a correspondence between the amount
of assistance researchers need and their receptivity to librarian involvement. The
different personas and levels of interest and need point to the wisdom of creating
services that offer varied levels of service, from providing basic data storage to
full-service metadata management.

Some qualities positively correlated with a researcher's receptivity to library
involvement in data management. These include a lack of existing support for
storage and preservation, a predisposition toward the open-access movement, and
a lack of support for management of data during the research process. The Colorado team also noted that earth science researchers seemed more open to library
involvement and data openness. Those in extremely competitive fields seemed to
be less receptive to library involvement in the data management process.

Although Lage and colleagues discovered a wide range of attitudes toward
data sharing and curation, there were some commonalities among many of the
researchers they talked to. Most researchers did not identify their data as public
data, though that did not necessarily mean they were not open to sharing it with
appropriate parties. Researchers often want to maintain some level of control over
their data, making individual determinations about when and with whom their
data is shared. Accordingly, receptivity to data repositories varies widely, often
depending on the level of control afforded the researcher by the repository. Talking to researchers about data governance issues gives them more confidence in
sharing their own data.

The Colorado interviews also revealed that few researchers are aware of depart-
mental procedures or services for storing data, that most researchers have some
subsets of research data that are not currently being maintained or preserved
with a plan in place, and that the tasks that go into effective data management
are perceived as burdensome distractions from their research projects. These
attitudes reveal that it is important to make data management as seamless and

painless as possible for researchers, and planning in advance can go a long way in that direction.

SO WHERE DO YOU START?

First, talk to your liaison or reference librarians. They are a wonderful resource for learning more about the research departments on campus. Get them involved early on, and have some discussions about the departments and faculty with whom they are familiar. Find out what they know about the kind of work going on around campus, who is collecting data, how well it is (or isn't) being managed in different departments, and where you might be able to make the most headway. Working with the people who already have solid relationships with faculty can put you ahead of the game.

But what if your library is just starting to develop relationships with research faculty? Now is the time to meet with department heads. Set up as many meetings as you can to talk about department research. Find out what grant-funded projects are already ongoing and who is currently working on submitting research grants. Try to gauge which researchers and departments are receptive to working with partners, where people seem to need more or less assistance, and which fields are already engaged in data-sharing practices. Some fields, such as physics and geological sciences, have already made strides in data-sharing practices and have established subject repositories and data management practices. Lage, Losoff, and Maness point out that choosing intentionally to reach out to researchers who may be receptive to library involvement is a wise move, especially for a newly created service. Reach out to those who seem receptive as pilot partners.

This is also a great time to find out what kinds of resources individual departments provide for their researchers, such as department file servers, specialized software, and grant-writing assistance. Additionally, talk to people in your campus IT department about available resources. It is likely that the IT department offers backup services for campus servers and researcher data. You likely should work closely with IT as you begin to develop a set of data management services, so begin developing a solid working relationship with them early on. Having good allies in campus technology services is often invaluable.

TALKING TO RESEARCHERS

Once you have identified researchers who are receptive to working with the library and who request assistance with a data management plan or data curation services, you move on to conduct data interviews specifically about their research projects. The data interview can be guided by the data management plan outline as well as by the research data lifecycle (see chapter 1). Find out before your data interview what the data management requirements are for their particular grant application, and use those requirements to guide your conversation. If there are no clear requirements, use the questions in chapter 3 of this guide to structure your interview.

Begin by asking researchers to describe their research projects. What questions are they trying to answer? What evidence will they be looking for? Who are their research partners, and who will be working on the project with them? Are their primary collaborators working from the same location? Are they from a public institution or private industry? Who will be gathering data? What is the anticipated term of the project? Try to get the big picture view of the research project.

Once you have a sense of the scope of the work, find out more about the specific data being gathered. What type of data will be collected? What processes will the data go through during the course of the research project, and what tools will be used to collect, process, and analyze the data? How much data do the researchers anticipate gathering? How fast will the data grow, and are there any changes it might undergo over time? Are they using any historical data or external data sources? Where will this data come from? Is it licensed, and what are the license limitations and stipulations?

When you know what tools will be used to gather data, you can find out specifics about file formats, naming conventions, and data storage plans. Where is data going to be stored? Will it be backed up? Who should have access to the data? Should there be a common file naming convention for all project participants? How will data elements be named and understood within files? Will data elements have identifiers?

This is often where metadata schemas come into play. In some research fields there are widely known and used metadata schemas, but not in all. You may want to familiarize yourself with metadata schemas used in the field in which the researchers work; chapter 5 of this guide helps give you a better sense of how to talk about metadata with researchers.

Data storage is an important component to address. Who is responsible for data backup and storage? Being aware of the options for data backup available to researchers on your campus is useful here, as is awareness of the pros and cons of different storage and backup options. If external hard drives will be used as the primary storage medium, they can fail, and they require more work to maintain on the part of the researcher. Cloud storage options can be relatively inexpensive, but researchers may sacrifice data privacy, and access to data is dependent on access to a network connection. Online backup services are a relatively good option but can be more expensive. And though they may be more secure than simple cloud storage like Dropbox or Google Docs, there is still the possibility of security failures. To learn more about storage options, talk to campus IT and find out what they recommend. Good data management is not just about selecting a storage option; it is also about policies, best practices, and support for backup and storage.[4]

You also must understand who owns and controls the data and whether there are privacy concerns. Does the funder have requirements for publishing data, and if so how will privacy concerns be addressed? How long will the data be retained? If access to the data will be provided, on what terms will it be provided? How do researchers typically disseminate their research results and data sets? What practices has the researcher followed in the past?

In many instances, researchers do not have ready answers to the questions you ask. Make note of their uncertainties so that you can search out the best answers for them. In most instances you will want to arrange a follow-up meeting to talk about what you have learned and walk them through their options. Think of yourself as a consultant, providing them an array of options and helping them make the best choices for their research project.

Where librarians can really be useful for researchers is in helping them go beyond the immediate answers to these questions. Librarians have unique skills in understanding organizational systems and thinking about organizing disparate information in order to ensure accessibility. Think deeply about the data the researcher talks about and the relationships between these pieces of data. If you are unfamiliar with the data that will be part of the research project, find reference sources such as encyclopedias and handbooks that can help you better understand the tools being used, the context of the research, and the data formats the researcher will be using.

It might be useful to talk, too, with the lab manager for the project, or the person who maintains any instruments used in data gathering. This person can help you understand how the data is generated or gathered. Garritano and Carlson suggest mapping out the workflow involved in gathering data, including the processing and analytical steps undertaken after data is gathered.[5] It might be useful to talk about this workflow with the people who are directly gathering data, if they are not the principle investigator on the project. Peters and Dryden point out that "the PI and his or her support staff are not always on the same page about what type of data is generated in any given study. . . . efforts should be made to interview multiple members of a project team."[6] Reach out to the students, lab assistants, and postdocs on the project team to gain a full picture of the research process.

You can also help researchers make connections with others on campus or in their disciplinary community who can provide support, tools, and information. This is where your research skills and ability to find information come in handy. Even if you do not currently know all the repositories or metadata standards in an obscure field, you can find the answers with a little sleuthing. This can be an invaluable service to busy researchers and helps you build up your arsenal of knowledge for working with researchers in the future as well.

The key to conducting an effective data interview is to listen closely to what the researchers say, and to help them think of things they have not yet considered. Once you are familiar with what goes into data management, from planning and metadata management to long-term preservation, you will be more aware of components they might leave out and can bring these up during the planning process to ensure they are being considered.

Additionally, you can help connect researchers with the resources that can enable them to practice good data management. This is where your network of campus and community contacts is key. You can do the groundwork and make researchers aware of what is available to them.

A data interview might be a one-off conversation or a series of consultations. You may offer a simple template for constructing a data management plan, or work closely with researchers to find answers to tough questions, or help them provision the resources they will need through the research data lifecycle. The extent of services you choose to offer around the creation and execution of data management plans varies, but whatever services you offer you should always begin with an information-gathering interview.

NOTES

1. Jake Carlson, "Demystifying the Data Interview: Developing a Foundation for Reference Librarians to Talk with Researchers about Their Data," *Reference Services Review* 40, no. 1 (October 2, 2012): 7–23.

2. Ibid.

3. Kathryn Lage, Barbara Losoff, and Jack Maness, "Receptivity to Library Involvement in Scientific Data Curation: A Case Study at the University of Colorado Boulder," *Portal: Libraries and the Academy* 11 (2011): 915–937.

4. See Florian Diekmann, "Data Practices of Agricultural Scientists: Results from an Exploratory Study," *Journal of Agricultural and Food Information* 13, no. 1 (2012): 14–34.

5. Jeremy R. Garritano and Jake R. Carlson, "A Subject Librarian's Guide to Collaborating on e-Science Projects," *Issues in Science and Technology Librarianship,* no. 57 (Spring 2009): 5.

6. C. Peters and A. R. Dryden, "Assessing the Academic Library's Role in Campus-Wide Research Data Management: A First Step at the University of Houston," *Science and Technology Libraries* 30 (2011): 387–403, 393 (quote).

Metadata

Researchers are almost uniformly confused by the term *metadata*. Jake Carlson at Purdue University writes, "Researchers have varying degrees of understanding about metadata, but often do not have a sense of what metadata should be applied to their data set to enable it to be discovered, understood, administered, or used by others."[1] Not only are they confused by it, they generally don't care much about it, either. Researchers are primarily interested in conducting their research, writing, sharing their work, and reading relevant research by others in their fields. Learning about metadata, implementing a useful schema, and creating high-quality metadata for collected research data are usually considered secondary to a researcher's primary work. Nevertheless, good metadata makes a researcher's primary work easier in the long run and enables researchers to find and use available data more easily.

Librarians are metadata experts. We have been using a variety of metadata schemas to organize library resources and make them available to a diverse group of users. We can use the knowledge we already possess about metadata and information organization to help researchers create useful metadata for their own research, but we need to familiarize ourselves with the metadata schemas in use in the fields in which our researchers work. We also need to learn to talk to researchers about metadata in ways that simplify and demystify metadata practices.

Metadata is, quite simply, structured information about things. Established metadata schemas bring standardization to a research project, but metadata does not necessarily have to be created using an existing schema, as long as it is internally consistent and provides all the information needed to understand the data. Librarians have been creating information about things for centuries, through our cataloging practices. The past decades have seen an explosion of metadata formats and schemas, as digital objects and digital data proliferate. You may already be familiar with metadata schemas that are widely used in libraries: Dublin Core, the Metadata Objects Description Schema (MODS), Encoded Archival Description (EAD), the Metadata Encoding and Transmission Standard (METS), and of course machine-readable cataloging (MARC). There are many other schemas in use in other fields, including Darwin Core in the biological sciences, Ecological Metadata Language (EML) in the ecological sciences, the Content Standard for Digital Geospatial Metadata (CSDGM), and the Text Encoding Initiative (TEI) in the humanities, social sciences, and linguistics, among others.

Using an established metadata schema to describe a data set improves the interoperability of the data. This means that data can be used in different systems and for different purposes, because it has been structured and defined in a way that is well understood by the user community. In some instances, metadata can be cross-walked to another schema, which also improves interoperability. Using an established schema ensures that people in the wider community can understand and use the data set more easily.

If interoperability is not reason enough to convince a researcher that metadata is important, explain that it can also improve the researcher's own usability of a particular data set. Applying a metadata schema to a data set ensures that the data is described consistently. It also ensures that the context and meaning of the data are discoverable to the researcher in the future.

Finally, high-quality metadata enables a data set to be discovered and preserved more easily. It is necessary for those who are looking for the data in a repository or other data system, and to help those who are managing digital data over the long run to ensure that the data set does not degrade over time or become unusable when software and hardware are changed or updated.

There are three different types of metadata that serve different purposes in describing a data set: descriptive metadata, administrative metadata, and structural metadata. Whether you need all three for a given data set depends on the data itself and the researcher's needs, both short and long term.

DESCRIPTIVE METADATA

Descriptive metadata is what you probably think of when you hear the term *metadata*. It is metadata that describes the object in question. In the case of research data, there are two levels of descriptive metadata to consider. One level describes the data set as a whole, and the other describes each element in the data set. Different schemas are used for these two types of descriptive metadata, and selecting a schema is informed by the research and the field.

The first level of metadata, describing the data set, should capture the purpose of the data and what it describes, who created it and when, what tools were used to gather the data, and any other information that applies to the entire data set. This information gives the data set a context and helps anyone who is reviewing the data understand its scope. Which information is important to gather depends on the research itself as well as where the data might be deposited.

Using an intended repository as a guide can be a useful way to create data set metadata. Many data repositories expect researchers to fill in some basic information about their data. If you know where researchers will deposit their work, check out the repository ahead of time and determine which metadata will be required when the data is deposited. If there is not a particular repository in mind, the use of the Dublin Core metadata elements is often a good default.

Dublin Core offers a set of "core" metadata elements for generic resource descriptions. Dublin Core has been widely adopted and allows for application interoperability with applications using Dublin Core or offering a mapping to Dublin Core. For example, the Dryad Data Repository uses a metadata application profile that is based on Dublin Core. If a researcher does not know where data might be deposited, or what additional information is needed, Dublin Core's generic set of descriptive elements provides some important information about the data set.

Simple Dublin Core, the most basic set of elements, consists of fifteen elements designed to describe generic resources: title, subject, description, resource type (preferably from a controlled vocabulary), source, relation, coverage (e.g., a spatial location, temporal period, or jurisdiction), creator, publisher, contributor, rights, date, format, identifier, and language. Not all of these elements apply to every data set, but they provide a good foundation if a researcher is unsure what metadata is important to include. Additionally, Qualified Dublin Core has additional elements including audience, provenance, and rights holder.

Additionally, the DataCite Metadata Schema is growing in use as a set of core metadata elements used to identify and cite data for research purposes.[2] The

DataCite Metadata Schema is used when registering identifiers through DataCite, and, like Dublin Core, it is made up of core and additional optional properties. There are only five mandatory properties in the DataCite schema: identifier, creator, title, publisher, and publication year. Users can also specify resource type, size, format, rights, version information, and subject terminology, among other fields. The DataCite schema also includes two administrative properties that can be useful for tracking provenance and update information.

Some research fields have widely accepted metadata schemas, ranging from simple to complex, that should be implemented. Darwin Core, for biodiversity research data, is fairly well known and used. Darwin Core works like Dublin Core, offering interoperability and a relatively simple framework. It adds fields that are important in biodiversity research, and the type vocabulary encompasses typical data in biodiversity research, including specially coded occurrence, geographic, and specimen data.

EML is widely used in the field of ecology. It is designed as a collection of modules, which allows for flexibility in its use. It can be extended, as well, for new types of resources. The top-level module in EML is compatible with Dublin Core and offers interoperability with many different types of repositories. The EML-Dataset module describes general information about a data set like title, abstract, contact information, and purpose of the data. There are modules for access control, file format, and geographic and temporal qualities of data.

The Data Document Initiative (DDI) is used in the social and behavioral sciences. It is a metadata schema that is designed to be used throughout the lifecycle of research data. Like EML, DDI has a modular structure that allows researchers flexibility and can reflect their particular research project.

There are many different options for recording important research metadata. Knowing what will work best in any particular project requires some research into the community of practice and some time familiarizing yourself with metadata practices and expectations and with the form of data that is gathered during the course of a project. In addition, researchers should consider what information they need to know about this data in order to give it context. What is important to remember? Are there geographic coordinates associated with the location where data was gathered? Are dates significant? What are the things that apply to every record in the data set? Your data interview should inform your consideration of metadata and help you and the researcher know what information is most important to record.

The second level of descriptive metadata applies to the element level. These two levels are not always easily separable within a particular metadata schema, but it can be helpful to be aware that these are two components of descriptive metadata. Element-level metadata is the metadata that is important during the data-gathering process and is used to label each data point, or data element, being recorded. This would ideally be considered before data gathering begins. If there are relevant metadata schemas established in a particular research field, using these schemas increases the interoperability of a data set. Even if a standard schema is not going to be used, it is useful for researchers to establish a consistent set of data elements to be collected by everyone working on the project. Establishing a consistent schema for data elements allows everyone working on a project to track data the same way and makes it easier to work with the data later.

Researchers should also consider what symbols, abbreviations, and terms will be used when gathering data. If everyone working on a project uses the same terms and abbreviations, the data is easier to use and share, and to understand at a later date. Consistency in labeling ensures that all the data is understood by everyone on the project, even if participants leave the project.

Properly constructed descriptive metadata makes it easier to interpret data in the future. Researchers have talked about not being able to find or understand their own data after it was collected; good metadata alleviates this potential problem.[3] Encourage researchers to think about how data will be used, both during and after a project. These considerations should guide the choice of metadata created and gathered. Researchers also need to consider where and how metadata that pertains to a particular data set should be stored.

ADMINISTRATIVE METADATA

Administrative metadata is metadata that assists in preservation and future use of the data. This metadata allows a repository to manage the digital objects that hold the data and includes information at the scale of the digital file itself, not its content. Administrative metadata can also include information about intellectual property rights. This metadata comes into play in the "preserve" phase of the digital curation lifecycle; it helps repository managers ingest, preserve, and provide access to the data sets being deposited.

Administrative metadata generally contains information about when and how the file was created—specifically, what software and hardware were used to create the data. Information about the file type and data format should be included, along with the names and locations of files and any relevant identifiers.

Storing digital data involves a great deal of preservation work, to ensure that file formats remain accessible. Preservation of digital data is a topic that could fill a set of volumes, but it is important to know that administrative metadata is key to the successful preservation of digital objects and digital data.

METS has one of the most fully developed schemas for administrative metadata. It breaks out administrative data into four subparts: technical metadata, about the file format and creation; intellectual property and rights metadata, about data ownership and access rights; source metadata, which is largely used for files digitized from an original analog source and might not pertain to research data; and digital provenance metadata, which is used to track any changes the file undergoes during the data lifecycle and preservation process.

In addition to administrative metadata about the data set itself, there is some metadata that can be created about the metadata attached to the data set. You want future users to know when the metadata was created and updated, and by whom. This is especially pertinent for the administrative metadata pertaining to digital provenance. If a file was migrated to an updated file format, it is important to record not only that the file was changed, when and by whom, but that the metadata itself was updated. The chain of custody of a digital object should be part of the administrative metadata.

Another key to preserving the integrity of digital objects is to include fixity information. Fixity information can support data integrity checks at the level of content data objects, using things like checksums and digital signatures that highlight any changes made to a file on the bit level.[4] This fixity information ensures that data has not been changed in an interim period of time and provides evidence of the integrity of data.

As data is more widely shared, intellectual property information is becoming increasingly important. There are several vocabularies for expressing rights to digital data. The most commonly known is Creative Commons, a set of tools that allows creators to provide certain types of access to their creations, including data sets. METS also includes a rights declaration schema, and other types of rights expressions are open-digital rights language, XrML (extensible rights markup language), and XACML (extensible access control markup language).

STRUCTURAL METADATA

Structural metadata is related to administrative metadata in that it is primarily used to preserve and provide continued access to digital data. Structural metadata describes the physical and logical structure of a digital object. This kind of metadata is important when there are multiple related files that must operate in a particular relationship to each other, such as video and audio files that should be played in conjunction or an audio file that is paired with a text file. Digital books often require structural metadata to ensure that they can be assembled and read in the correct order.

The Digital Production and Integration Program at Yale University has created a best-practices document that outlines six levels of structural metadata that vary depending on the type of digital object to which the metadata is being applied.[5] Structural metadata is most commonly applied to digitized objects such as books and other paged text and image collections. The metadata enables viewing systems to display files in the correct order and enhances searching and discoverability.

METS packages together descriptive, administrative, and structural metadata for digital objects and is a good place to start exploring structural metadata. However, for research data, most data repositories can guide you in submitting data that is in multiple parts.

Preservation metadata can be a complicated topic; for a richer discussion of the types and uses of preservation metadata, see chapter 6.

METADATA SERVICES

Metadata services may be some of the most useful services librarians can provide researchers. As we noted earlier, researchers are not particularly interested in metadata creation and don't know much about it. Anna Gold suggests that metadata should be captured as a by-product of data production, but currently not all researchers use tools that allow for that data capture.[6] To help them identify tools and techniques that ease the process of metadata creation, we need to understand their data creation workflows and the metadata needs for their research. Additionally, data managers might work with computer scientists to use creative means to capture metadata from other sources such as proposals, abstracts, and publications.

Like most data management services, metadata services can range from more involved to less. You might choose to provide information to researchers about different metadata standards that are used in their research domains via a website or guide. You might offer trainings and workshops on those standards or just provide documentation on their use.

You could choose to work one-on-one with researchers to identify a metadata standard or schema that would work best for their research, or you might simply help them come up with consistent identification practices for their research data and use the organization tools they have to create meaningful metadata (e.g., researchers can use file names effectively to record important information about their data sets).

If you have more resources available, you might may be able to work with researchers to help them create metadata during the research project, whether descriptive or administrative. You may even be able to create simple web applications or online tutorials that will aid them in the process of creating metadata.[7]

As with every other aspect of your services, you should work with researchers and assess your own resources to craft the level of services that best meet the needs of everyone involved. But having an understanding of the types of metadata researchers might need or want to create helps you work more effectively with them, no matter what services you are offering.

NOTES

1. Jake Carlson, "Demystifying the Data Interview: Developing a Foundation for Reference Librarians to Talk with Researchers about Their Data," *Reference Services Review* 40, no. 1 (October 2, 2012): 7–23, 17 (quote).

2. *DataCite Metadata Schema for the Publication and Citation of Research Data,* DataCite, March 2011, http://schema.datacite.org/meta/kernel-2.1/doc/DataCite -MetadataKernel_v2.1.pdf.

3. Dharma Akmon, Ann Zimmerman, Morgan Daniels, and Margaret Hedstrom, "The Application of Archival Concepts to a Data-Intensive Environment: Working with Scientists to Understand Data Management and Preservation Needs," *Archival Science* 11, no. 3/4 (November 2011): 329–348. doi:10.1007/s10502-011-9151-4.

4. "DCC Curation Lifecycle Model," Digital Curation Centre, www.dcc.ac.uk/resources/ curation-lifecycle-model.

5. *Best Practices for Structural Metadata,* Yale University Library, June 1, 2008, www .library.yale.edu/dpip/bestpractices/BestPracticesForStructuralMetadata.pdf.

6. Anna Gold, "Cyberinfrastructure, Data, and Libraries, Part 1," *D-Lib Magazine* 13, no. 9/10 (October 2007): 6. doi:10.1045/september20september-gold-pt1.

7. See Mark A. Parsons, Oystein Godoy, Ellsworth LeDrew, Taco F. de Bruin, Bruno Danis, Scott Tomlinson, and David Carlson, "A Conceptual Framework for Managing Very Diverse Data for Complex, Interdisciplinary Science," *Journal of Information Science* 37, no. 6 (2011): 555–569. doi:10.1177/0165551511412705.

Data Preservation

Whether or not researchers want to provide access to their research data, preserving that data is crucially important. Digital data has very different preservation requirements than physical collections of data, such as data gathered in lab notebooks, and many researchers are unaware of what needs to be done to ensure continued usability of their digital data. Researchers often misunderstand the concept of data preservation. Although *preservation* and *archiving* have fairly specific meanings for librarians, this is not always the case for those generating the data to be preserved. You should begin the discussion of data preservation by ensuring that stakeholders have a common understanding of the terms, and that you are all on the same page when talking about data preservation.

There are many things that go into effective preservation of research data, and ideally these factors are considered at the beginning of a research project. When you are planning for data management, it is critical to determine early on where the data will be stored long term and whether it will be archived in a repository. This ensures that any polices or procedures for archiving data are known and understood before the data is collected, and the researcher can therefore better organize and manage the data to ensure easy archiving later. It is crucial, though, that researchers consider preservation needs, no matter where in the research process they are.

STORAGE VERSUS PRESERVATION AND ARCHIVING

Data storage is simply that—placing the data somewhere it can be accessed if and when needed. Data might be stored on local internal or external hard drives, cloud-based systems, or servers. Storing the data does not, however, safeguard against some threats to it, such as media degradation or obsolescence of data formats, nor does it provide future access via a search interface. Data storage is likely already part of a researcher's work, but methods of data storage should be explicitly discussed and agreed upon at the beginning of a project. Work goes more smoothly if every partner in a research project uses the same data storage methods and is familiar with how and where all data is being stored.

Often, researchers keep data after the project is over in the same location it was stored during the research process, without considering how that might impact long-term usability and accessibility of the data. Archiving data means active preservation of the data as well as taking measures to increase its discoverability and accessibility. It involves, among other things, giving unique, persistent identifiers to data and performing common checks for corruption and replication.

A data archive (also called a center, repository, bank, or library) specializes in archiving data rather than simply storing it. One attribute common to data archives is the use of user-friendly digital systems, which are often web accessible. Archives or repositories provide an interface for data discovery and downloading and support identifiers that facilitate data citation.[1]

It is important for researchers to understand the difference between simple storage and proper archiving. If researchers leave digital data on servers or hard drives, without performing necessary preservation actions periodically, they will find that their data eventually becomes unusable.

REPOSITORY TYPES

Researchers should consider several factors when determining to which data archive or repository to submit their data: the data type, its potential future users, sensitivity and privacy issues, and its importance. By selecting an appropriate repository, the data is more likely to be discovered and reused in the future. Repositories may be either domain specific or institutional. Sometimes researchers opt to archive their data personally, but this comes with certain costs and obligations of which researchers may not be aware. In some cases, data may be archived in multiple repositories, including both domain and institutional.

Domain Repositories

Many research disciplines have repositories designed specifically for their domain's data types. Examples include eCrystals for x-ray crystallographic data (http://ecrystals.chem.soton.ac.uk), the National Oceanographic Data Center (NODC, www.nodc.noaa.gov), the Protein DataBank (www.pdb.org), which houses experimentally determined structures for protein and nucleic acids, and the Inter-university Consortium for Political and Social Research (ICPSR, www.icpsr.umich.edu). Often these domain repositories have analytical and discovery tools available alongside the data to encourage data reuse.

Some suggest that data should be housed solely in domain repositories.[2] They argue that domain repositories allow for the provision of specialized metadata, enhanced review and validation by experts in the field, and the ability to create specialized search and discovery tools as well as deposit and validation tools. However, not all disciplines have data repositories available, and data tends to be unique and idiosyncratic in nature, making some data unsuitable for existing repositories.

Green and Gutmann nicely summarize the strengths of domain repositories as follows:[3]

- Managers have knowledge of content, file types, migration and emulation strategies, research requirements, and analytical techniques.
- Preservation commitment is as important as access.
- Support services are well established.
- They have a commitment to supporting the quality of research.
- They are active at the national and international levels of funding, infrastructure planning, and data set production.
- Training and community building occurs across institutions, faculty, graduate students, and other archives.
- They are not controlled by local agendas.

Institutional Repositories

Repositories housed at the institutional level are intended to collect, manage, and maintain the intellectual output of a particular institution or group of institutions. The concept of institutional repositories gained immense popularity in the early 2000s, resulting in the establishment of software for these facilities such as DuraSpace's Fedora and the DSpace software, both software systems for implementing a repository. You may already be supporting an institutional repository through your library, or your campus IT department may offer this service. Perhaps you are considering establishing an institutional repository as part of a suite of data services.

The institutional repository is intended to be used as a repository for research articles, theses, data sets, administrative documents, course notes, and other digital assets. Many of these documents might be considered "gray" literature that would not likely be preserved without the existence of the institutional repository. Many institutions use this kind of repository as an archive for institutional records, and they are sometimes managed by the campus archives department.

Institutional repositories often serve as open-access ("OA Green") repositories by providing a way for researchers to self-archive all of their publications, regardless of the openness of the original journal that published the article. Many of the repositories in the Directory of Open Access Repositories (OpenDOAR) are institutional repositories. Green and Gutmann summarize the strengths of institutional repositories for researchers as follows:[4]

- Local contacts and support services are available.
- Open-access goals are pursued.
- Recent attention sometimes brings funding and staff resources.
- Preservation commitment may be strong, though it varies across institutions.

From a librarian's perspective, establishing an institutional repository can require a great deal of resources, in both personnel and infrastructure. Many librarians can tell you that simply installing open-source repository software and waiting for resources to be deposited is not a winning strategy. Gaining traction with an institutional repository requires a great deal of effort, not only in the actual maintenance of the software and the data deposited but in creating institutional buy-in. Outreach to and engagement of faculty are some of the greatest struggles librarians talk about when establishing an institutional repository . If you are considering a project like this, construct a solid implementation plan and do lots of research on best practices. Building a repository is a large project, and a full discussion is beyond the scope of this book. Appendix A points you to some excellent resources for creating an institutional repository.

Other Options

Although it is not advisable, some researchers choose to archive their data outside of a larger repository framework. This often takes the form of storing the data on a server or cloud-based storage. There is a noticeable trend in the commercialization of digital data storage and services.[5] Amazon's Cloud Drive and Microsoft Azure are both examples of these kinds of services. Researchers are increasingly using these services, then providing access to their data via their personal websites, project websites, or some other venue. Access to and discovery of the data depend on the researcher's ability to maintain the websites, as well as to perform proper backup and replication actions. Researchers using this method of preservation should be encouraged to submit their data to a public, curated repository with long-term sustainability. When you are talking with researchers about their preservation options, make sure they are aware of the types of things that must be done to ensure long-term accessibility of their digital files. Some of these types of necessary preservation actions are detailed later in this chapter.

PRESERVATION COSTS

Preserving data for the long term has a cost; although the infrastructure itself is costly, more significant is the cost associated with human resources, such as personnel to manage and maintain the archive. Storage costs for digital data are decreasing, but costs related to storage, such as power, data curation and annotation, and personnel, are not decreasing.[6] Increasing amounts of digital data, and the need to comply with regulations regarding backup and monitoring, emphasize that these costs should not be underestimated or overlooked.

Short-term costs for data preservation are primarily those related to storing data rather than archiving it. This may include software or hardware for backing up data or personnel costs for managing and organizing data for storage. Longer-term preservation costs are associated with archives. Many repositories and archives use annual pricing schemes for a set amount of data; this situation is changing, however, to better meet the needs of researchers whose costs are intertwined with grant cycles.

Both short-term and long-term costs should be outlined and justified in any data management plan created. Researchers should consider the institutional resources available to them at low or no cost.

THE PRESERVATION PROCESS

Data Appraisal

Today, there is not enough storage available for the digital data being produced, and the rate of digital data production is much faster than the production of storage capacity.[7] This implies that not all data can be kept, and therefore the first step to preserving data is to determine which data sets to keep. This determination is called *appraisal,* and it is necessary for all disciplines to engage in this discussion of data importance.[8] It is commonly agreed that any data underpinning publications should be archived and preserved for the long term. This is often called "the data behind the graphs," and preserving it ensures reproducibility and accountability in scientific research. Historically significant data should also be kept, along with unique data that is not reproducible.

Repository Selection

There are hundreds of repositories available for archiving data; selecting the most appropriate archiving locations should take place at the beginning of a research project. Considerations for repository selection include the fees charged (both current and projected), the services offered by the archive (e.g., replication, discovery), and the value and potential reusability of the data set. It may be appropriate to store data in multiple repositories. For example, all data from a project may be stored in an institutional repository, whereas subsets of that data may also be stored in domain-specific repositories to enhance discoverability. You can assist researchers in this decision-making process by researching the options available to them and guiding them to make a meaningful appraisal of their data.

Document and Deposit Data

Data documentation should take place throughout the life of the project. Chapter 5 can help you guide researchers to create the most useful metadata and documentation from the beginning of their research projects. If metadata is being created throughout the project lifecycle, data deposit is easier. Considering which repositories might be candidates for deposit can give guidance for metadata creation; even so, metadata may need to be reformatted or edited for deposit in particular repositories. Depositing the metadata and data into a repository is the final step in ensuring that the data is preserved for the long term.

PRESERVATION BEHIND THE SCENES

From a library or archive perspective, a great deal more goes into the preservation process. Preservation requires its own set of metadata and other information that is not of much interest to a researcher but is essential for effective digital preservation.

For those managing data long term, there are metadata needs and considerations other than those of researchers. Unlike traditional paper records, digital records require computer mediation via hardware and software, and the rapid pace of change in the digital world means those technologies come and go quickly. To meet the challenge of digital preservation, you must be equipped with an arsenal of carefully kept information about each digital object in an archive. That information can go a long way to ensuring that digital objects do not become obsolete along with the technologies used to create them.

The metadata associated with preserving digital objects, which is sometimes called administrative metadata and sometimes preservation metadata, can be roughly broken into two types: *description information* and *representation information*. The boundaries between these two types of metadata are not stable, and overlap is inevitable due to the nature of the information, but conceptualizing preservation metadata needs through these two categories can make it easier for repository managers and archivists to do the work of preservation effectively. Description information and representation information play roles in every stage of the preservation, or data curation, lifecycle, from the creation of a digital object, to its dissemination to the repository's users (its *designated community*), to its eventual transformation (or disposal). Without complete and well-maintained description and representation information, long-term preservation of digital objects would be impossible.

The general form of description and representation information comes from the Open Archival Information System (OAIS) reference model, in which each category of information is broken down into further categories.[9] The OAIS model allows flexibility; individual archives and repositories can select which metadata schemes they use to fulfill the information requirements. Description and representation information can be seen as two sides of the digital preservation coin. Description information provides the metadata needed for preservation, including information related to the history of the digital object and its context within the archive. Representation information, which can also be considered structural metadata, is the metadata associated with rendering a digital object accurately and maintaining all necessary components for its use by the archive's designated community. Both sets of metadata combine to ensure the longevity and continued usefulness of digital objects that would otherwise be rendered a stream of meaningless bits.

Representation information is usually described as comprising two components, *structure information* and *semantic information*. Structure information deals specifically with the digital bit sequences of a data object. It tells the data curator (and users) about file formats, software and hardware, and other technical information necessary to render a digital object. Semantic information describes how those values should be interpreted.[10] It includes such things as the headers on a spreadsheet, the units of measurement in a data set, and the language in which a text document was written.

How do repository managers and archivists determine what and how much information to keep about a particular data object? How does one know what will be important, what the future community of users will know and not know, need and not need? To make decisions about how much information to preserve, each data object is analyzed to determine its *significant properties* and its *underlying abstract form.*

A data object's significant properties are those elements of a data object that are important for its usefulness to the designated community. For example, a spreadsheet that contains automatic calculations might need to have those calculations (the spreadsheet's behaviors) preserved, whereas an article in PDF form with hyperlinked URLs in the references section might not need the hyperlinks themselves to be preserved, since the external URLs might change and the references contain enough information in themselves to continue to be useful for researchers.

There are five types of information that together make up an object's significant properties: content, context, appearance, structure, and behavior. The elements that need to be preserved in each of these five areas might be different for different types of documents and different designated communities. Content information relates to the intellectual content of the object, context information to the object's relationships with other objects and other intellectual content or communities. Appearance information includes things like color, layout, and font size. Structure information tells the user about things like pagination, embedded files, and headings, and behavior relates to how a document works, including things like hyperlinks and calculations. Some elements of a document may be more important than others, but all have to be determined for each object within the context of the designated community's knowledge base and needs. And all of these pieces of information are used to preserve and render the digital object's underlying abstract form.

The concept of the underlying abstract form (UAF) rests on the idea that data has an existence separate from the medium on which it is written. To preserve a data object effectively, one first must discover which elements, which significant properties, are essential to maintain the highest level of abstraction of the data without losing any important information or function.

Many digital objects are created in common file formats, which leads to the potential for a great amount of replication of labor in creating representation information. To avoid some of this replication, many archives and digital preservation project groups are beginning to construct representation information registries. These registries exist to provide centralized, locatable, and systematic representation information for common types of digital objects. The benefits of this kind of knowledge sharing among the digital preservation community are tremendous; the creation of metadata for individual objects can be more automated and more efficient, as well as more sustainable, because of its redundancy and separation from individual data objects in an archive. The groups creating these registries include the Cedars Distributed Archive Prototype Demonstrator, the PRONOM Technical Registry, the Digital Curation Centre's Representation Information Registry Repository, and the National Geospatial Data Archive Format Registry.

Representation information is significant in all phases of the preservation lifecycle. Ideally, when an object is being created the creator maintains information about the format in which the object was created, the operating system and software being used, and the meaning of the content and context. When a digital object is being appraised for inclusion in a repository or digital archive, the archivist might determine that the specific file formats are not able to be included at that time, or that an object might need to be migrated to a different file format. When a data set and its metadata are being put together for ingest, representation information must be included as part of the overall information package. Representation information is used during the ingest process to determine if any initial actions must take place for immediate use and preservation, and to clarify relationships between digital objects.

During a digital object's lifetime within an archive, various preservation events may take place periodically to ensure continued access to that object. Representation information helps archivists determine when and if preservation events must take place. Finally, representation information helps end users know how to access a data set. It should contain information about what software or emulators to use, or it might include the software or emulator itself, but without that knowledge a user would have no way to know how to access or use the information object.

Representation information is not all that is needed to preserve digital objects effectively. Description information is an essential piece of the preservation process. If representation information is used to translate a digital object, description

55

information is used to maintain a record of every action taken toward the creation and preservation of that object. The OCLC/RLG Working Group on Preservation Metadata writes, "Preservation Description Information, while also encompassing static properties, emphasizes the temporal aspects of the object, extending from its creation, to its ingest into the digital archive, to its retention in the archival store."[11] Description information consists of four categories: *reference data, context data, provenance data,* and *fixity data.*

Reference information is metadata related to the identity of a digital object. Each digital object must be given a persistent identifier to enable the designated community to access that object and to enable the repository system, as well as other global systems, to identify and refer to the object. The reference information should include not just the particular object's ID but further information about how that ID is constructed and who is responsible for the construction. Reference information can also include metadata for resource description and discovery, such as metadata created at the time of the object's creation or created by the archivist on ingest, including MARC or Dublin Core records.

Context information defines the relationship of the digital object to its environment. This is slightly different from the context relationships defined as a significant property of a document in the representation information. That form of context information defines relationships between intellectual objects and the context in which they were created and should be used. The context information related to description describes the digital relationships between objects—whether other manifestations of the object exist, and whether there are other intellectually related objects within the repository. Admittedly, there is some overlap between these two types of context information, but the primary purpose of description context information is to ensure that related objects are kept together and that any preservation events do not permanently separate them or destroy their ability to work together. The OCLC/RLG Working Group describes the difference between these types of context information succinctly: "Description and Context Information is directed at informational requirements associated with managing the preservation process, not those aimed at facilitating the understanding and interpretation of the Content Data Object's intellectual content."[12] Each piece of context information should include the relationship type as well as any identifiers that help to maintain the relationships.

Provenance information might be the most crucial element of description information. It contains a record of every action that has been taken in regards to the digital object, from its creation to its storage in the archival system. Provenance information revolves around the idea of the *event,* and digital objects can be seen as part of an evolutionary preservation process. A record should be kept whenever a digital object is migrated, moved, or undergoes a transfer of ownership—in short, whenever the digital object undergoes any kind of change. Provenance information helps to ensure that the significant properties of an object are being preserved through its lifecycle.

Provenance information can be clearly broken down into lifecycle stages. It should be created when the object is created, whenever any changes are made to it prior to being ingested into an archive, upon ingest, and whenever a preservation action is taken. This information should also include data about permissions and legal rights at each stage of the lifecycle. For each stage, metadata should include information about what was done (including descriptions), the date on which is was done, who did it, and the outcome of the event.

The final component of description information, fixity data, is provided to verify electronically that the bit stream of a digital object is unchanged. It is used to ensure the authenticity of an object—that the object in the archive is what it purports to be and has not been damaged or significantly changed by any of the preservation events undertaken. There are a variety of verification methods for digital objects, including MD5 checksums, watermarks, digital signatures, hash encryption, and private keys. These require software, and the fixity information should include not just the verification key itself but data about the software and procedures used to create that key. Each time data is authenticated, a record should be kept noting the date and result of the authentication.

Description information, by its very nature, plays a role in every stage of the preservation lifecycle. Its purpose is to document that lifecycle itself and to ensure that accurate records exist for every action taken in relation to that object.

Neither representation nor description information alone is adequate for effective long-term preservation of digital objects, and there are often spaces where the metadata from each category may overlap. At times, it may seem unnecessary or messy to try to separate these types of metadata, but being able to conceptualize these two categories and their separate roles in the preservation process can help archivists be sure they are preserving all the necessary metadata alongside the digital object to ensure its continued usefulness.

PRESERVATION SERVICES

The preservation services your library offers, like most other data services, can range from more to less involved. You might want to offer information about methods of preservation and significant domain repositories that are available to researchers. You might opt to offer a depositing service, where the library manages the deposit of data sets into appropriate repositories on behalf of researchers. Or you might decide to implement an institutional repository or collaborate to create a domain repository.

Preservation of digital data requires its own specialized knowledge and set of tasks. It is not enough to simply store data; specific actions must be taken to ensure its continued usability and accessibility. If you choose to implement a local repository, be sure you and your team understand what the software you choose can do and what additional work you are taking on. Long-term preservation of data is a big commitment; be sure that you have the resources you need to be a trustworthy partner in the data preservation arena.

NOTES

1. "Archiving Your Research Data," Johns Hopkins University Data Management Services, http://dmp.data.jhu.edu/assistance/archiving-your-research-data.

2. For example, see "Repositories for Scientific Data," petermr's blog, Unilever Cambridge Centre for Molecular Informatics, http://blogs.ch.cam.ac.uk/pmr/2010/07/28/pp4_01-repositories-for-scientific-data/.

3. Ann Green, and Myron Gutmann, "Preserving Things That Count: Exploring Partnerships among Domain Specific Repositories, Institutional Repositories, and Social Science Researchers," Inter-university Consortium for Political and Social Research, 2006, access via http://ecommons.cornell.edu/handle/1813/3692.

4. Ibid.

5. F. Berman, "Got Data? A Guide to Data Preservation in the Information Age," *Communications of the ACM* 51, no. 12 (2008): 50–56.

6. Ibid.

7. Ibid.

8. Angus Whyte and Jonathan Tedds, "Making the Case for Research Data Management," *DCC Briefing Papers,* 2011, www.dcc.ac.uk/resources/briefing-papers/making-case-rdm.

9. *The Consultative Committee for Space Data Systems, Reference Model for an Open Archival Information System (OAIS),* June 2012, http://public.ccsds.org/publications/archive/650x0m2.pdf.

10. See Adrian Brown, *Representation Information Registries,* Planets project website, www.planets-project.eu/docs/reports/Planets_PC3-D7_RepInformationRegistries.pdf.

11. OCLC/RLG Working Group on Preservation Metadata, *A Metadata Framework to Support the Preservation of Digital Objects,* OCLC, June 2002, www.oclc.org/research/projects/pmwg/pm_framework.pdf, 30.

12. Ibid., 39.

Access

Providing access to research data can be thought of as the final step in data management. Before access can be granted to others, the data must be well documented, properly organized and stored, adequately licensed, and preserved for the long term. These steps are necessary predecessors of providing access. Also necessary is obtaining a persistent, unique identifier for the dataset (e.g., a digital object identifier, or DOI). Data without this identifier may be minimally accessible but cannot be properly referenced or cited, which is a major incentive for data sharing.

Libraries can provide a range of roles in the provision of access to research data, and there are many services we can offer to researchers to help them determine the best access options for their data. Some libraries support institutional repositories, directly providing access to research data produced at their institutions, but this might not be the best option for your library. You might choose instead to offer consultation services to researchers, to help them locate the best domain repositories for their work, or even to submit research data on behalf of researchers. To determine the ways you can be most effective, talk with researchers to determine what they need and what options are available in their fields. You also need to assess your own resources to know how you and your staff can best be of service.

The level of data access that might be given for any particular data set ranges from completely closed and unavailable to fully open. On the closed end of this spectrum, data may be available only to the investigators involved in the study;

this type of closed data may be required in cases where security and confidentiality of the data set are important. On the open end, data is freely available in the public domain for all to use. In between these two ends of the spectrum, data may be available to colleagues on a request basis. See chapter 8 on data governance to consider the appropriate licenses.

Many institutions and funders are now requiring that research data be deposited and made accessible, for example, in an institutional data repository. Most institutions have official policies on retention and access to research data that address issues such as protection of and access to sensitive data as well as offering guidelines for investigators who are leaving the institution on how best to provide access to their data.[1] Some journals are mandating access to data that underlies articles they publish; this ensures reproducibility and the credibility of their publications. The Dryad Data Repository has partnered with many journals in the life sciences to provide unfettered access to data that supports articles they publish.[2]

Once you have buy-in from higher-level administrators at your institution, you may want to propose an institutional data policy. An institutional data policy can help to protect institutional data while ensuring that it remains accessible and useful for members of the institution. A policy can help clarify questions of data ownership and give guidance to researchers in the context of licensing issues. It can also protect the personal information of members of the university community, when research involves gathering sensitive information. These policies lay out the rights and responsibilities of researchers on campus.

When you are crafting an institutional policy, get the input of stakeholders including members of the institutional review board and heads of research departments and programs. Be sure to differentiate between administrative institutional data and research data gathered by institutional researchers. The two require some different policies and regulations.

Research data management policies generally include statements strongly encouraging or requiring that research projects include a data management plan. They may state what the institution will provide (backup mechanisms, data storage, guidance and training) and may require or encourage deposit or registration in an institutional repository. They should outline the rights and responsibilities of researchers regarding their data and make clear how the institution views ownership and copyright issues related to data and research. There are many online sources of guidance on crafting institutional and research data policies, such as the excellent examples at the University of Edinburgh, Ohio State University, and Stanford University.[3]

THE ROLE OF IDENTIFIERS

Unique, persistent identifiers for research data are critical to providing access to that data. Researchers are often aware of DOIs because these have been used to identify research publications for some time. They may not, however, realize that data sets can also receive these identifiers, which allows them to be cited easily and their usage statistics tracked. When helping a researcher select the best identifier scheme, keep in mind that public data identifiers should be "actionable" (i.e., you can click on them in a web browser), globally unique, persistent. These characteristics imply that data identifiers should have corresponding online resolver services (e.g., http://dx.doi.org for DOIs) and remain actionable over the long term. Most important, metadata associated with the identifier (including the physical location of the data) must be kept up-to-date to avoid a user encountering error messages when trying to locate a dataset.

Data citation has received significant attention in recent years, partly via the DataCite organization (www.datacite.org), based in Europe. DataCite is a consortium of libraries, publishers, funders, and other stakeholders interested in facilitating data access via persistent identifiers. Persistent identifiers are not limited to DOIs, however. Many museums and repositories have developed their own identifier systems. Examples include MuseumID (http://museumid.net) for museum specimens and samples and Archival Resource Keys (ARKs, https://confluence .ucop.edu/display/Curation/ARK) from the California Digital Library.

Because persistent identifiers tend to be opaque (e.g., a string of digits) and to reveal little or nothing about the nature of the identified object, it is also important for researchers to maintain metadata associated with the data set. Among the most important pieces of metadata to maintain is the target URL that ensures that the identifier remains actionable. Here are some commonly used identifier schemes:[4]

- ARK (archival resource key): URL with extra features allowing you to ask for descriptive and archival metadata and to recognize certain kinds of relationships between identifiers. It is used by memory organizations such as libraries, archives, and museums.[5]
- DOI (digital object identifier): identifier that becomes actionable when embedded in a URL. It has become popular in academic journal publishing, but use is spreading to data sets via DataCite.[6]
- Universally unique identifier (UUID): identifier whose purpose is to enable distributed organizations to provide identifiers without significant central

coordination. UUIDs are often called "practically unique" rather than guaranteed unique.[7]

There are also discipline- and domain-specific identifier schemes:

- InChI (IUPAC international chemical identifier): identifier for chemical substances that can be used in printed and electronic data sources, thus enabling easier linking of diverse data compilations[8]
- LSID (life sciences identifier): identifier used for biologically significant resources, including species names, concepts, occurrences, genes or proteins, or data objects that encode information about them[9]
- NCBI (National Center for Biotechnology Information) Accession: nonactionable number in use by the NCBI[10]

All persistent identifiers need resolvers; that is, the identifier must be able to be tracked back to the actual digital object. The identifier frequently points to a target URL that leads directly to the object. The process of getting to the final target is called *resolution*. Resolution on the web is usually fast and invisible. It is done behind the scenes on your behalf by web browsers. Unsuccessful resolution, however, usually means visible failure to access the object you were expecting, resulting in a "broken identifier." Objects tend to move, so identifier persistence depends on resolution using up-to-date target URLs. As an example, a URL can be created using the DOI resolver (based at www.doi.dx.org) and the DOI assigned to a data set or document. If the owner of the document or data set keeps the DOI resolver up-to-date when the location of the data changes, the doi.dx.org URL always resolves to the correct end location of the data set or document.

Libraries interested in providing identifiers to their researchers have two main options. One is to have an independent identifier service, run locally, using open-source software. This is a good option if your library has technical resources available to set up this service and run it properly. For example, UUIDs can be generated locally at the library via open-source software (UUID Generator). The second option is to partner with an organization that provides identifiers. This may be another library, a consortium of libraries, or an organization such as EZID (www.cdlib.org/services/uc3/ezid), which is a member of DataCite and based at the California Digital Library.

THE BENEFITS OF ACCESS

Providing access to data benefits researchers, their institutions, their funders, and the public. First, providing access to the data that underlies a publication or research result ensures reproducibility of those results. This is one of the foundations of academic research; if results are not reproducible, they do not endure over time and contribute to the progress of the field. Access to underlying data also lends credibility to both the researcher and the results being reported. This credibility extends to the institution and the funders as well. If data is made available to other researchers for use, the speed at which research progresses accelerates. Redundant data collection is less likely, and data that is expensive or difficult to collect can be reused and repurposed. Institutions and funders receive maximum gain for their investment, and the public benefits from the faster pace of research.

Whyte and Pryor surveyed the literature and compiled a list of advantages to making research data open and accessible; their list closely matches the advantages stated above.[11] They note that open, accessible data benefits the speed and efficiency of the research cycle, including economic benefits that result from researchers collaborating rather than working separately on similar projects. Additionally, open data results in capabilities for identifying new research questions, especially those that combine many digital data sets for meta-analysis.[12] They observe as well that research effectiveness and quality are improved with open access; researchers consider a result more reputable if the underlying data is shared alongside the published article. Innovation, knowledge exchange, and impact of research are also enhanced by open access. Louis and colleagues examined the relationship between commercial industries in the United States and academia, citing the benefits to society of biomedical research sharing between these groups.[13] Finally, in Whyte and Pryor's list, a researcher's career development is positively affected by open access to research data, primarily because of its contribution to the previous four advantages. Researchers who participate in open exchange of ideas and data are seen as good stewards of the scientific process.

The most important benefit to researchers in making their data accessible is the capability of receiving credit for all aspects of their research, including the data they collect. This should be emphasized in conversations with researchers about data accessibility. Piwowar and colleagues showed that sharing research data for a publication leads to an increased citation rate of that publication.[14] Since

65

publications and their citation are the currency of achievement in research, this is a strong argument for researchers to share their data openly and provide easy access.

RESTRICTING ACCESS

Although restricting access to data is not ideal in most situations, some data sets require it.[15] The most common reason for restricting access is that the data set has information related to individuals (i.e., research on human subjects). Precautions should be taken to make such data anonymous, but even then it may still be necessary to restrict access. There also may be economic, political, or security risks that necessitate restricted access to data; geospatially linked data related to endangered species, humans, or sensitive habitats are all examples. A third justification for restricting data access involves issues of intellectual property; data associated with a project that has commercial potential, for example, may need special protections. Finally, if researchers are not the primary owners of the data set (i.e., third-party data), they may not have the permissions necessary to provide access to the data.

OPEN ACCESS

Open-access content has three basic characteristics: it is digital, free to access, and available online. There are no price or permission barriers, the full content is available, and it is made available immediately. Providing unfettered access to research data is compatible with the open-access movement and is often referred to as "open data." The idea behind the open-data movement is that certain data should be freely available to everyone to use and republish as they wish, without restrictions from copyright, patents, or other mechanisms of control. To guarantee that data is open, researchers must deliberately place their data in the public domain, for example, with a Creative Commons (CC-0) license Zero.[16]

SELECTING A REPOSITORY AND SUBMITTING DATA

Thousands of repositories are available for researchers to deposit their data and provide access to it. The selection of the most appropriate repository should take into account several questions:

- Who will need access to this data set in the future? Where will they be likely to look for it?
- Is there an appropriate discipline-specific repository or subject repository for the dataset?
- What are the access policies for the repository? Is there flexibility in who can have access to the data, or when the data can be made available?
- What is the repository's sustainability plan? How long will it keep the data and provide access?
- Does the repository take any type of data, or are there format restrictions?
- What metadata standard does the repository require?

To narrow the search for the appropriate repository, consult lists of repositories such as DataBib (http://databib.org) or re3data.org (http://re3data.org), both curated list of repositories that can be searched via keyword.

The process for submitting data to the repository selected varies widely. Researchers should consult the repository's website when preparing their data. Most repositories have a "Frequently Asked Questions" web page or a step-by-step guide for depositing data. Data submission sometimes takes the form of a web-based upload system, or researchers may submit their data directly to the curator via e-mail for deposition. You may wish to provide assistance to researchers with data deposit or offer step-by-step instructions for some common repositories via library guides. Look at repository websites to find out whether they already offer these kinds of resources and whether you can make them available to your users.

INSTITUTIONAL REPOSITORIES

In many libraries, thinking about establishing data services immediately leads to a call for an institutional repository. The open-source software that is widely available for running a repository makes this seem like a compelling proposition; if you have someone reasonably tech savvy on your team, you can install a repository and have it up and running in a matter of days. But this seeming ease belies the fact that a successful repository requires significant planning, thought, energy, and, yes, money. A successful institutional repository should be part of an overall data services strategy.[17]

For many librarians and campus administrators, an institutional repository is framed as a tool to showcase institutional research. But the institutional repository is not just a tool for collecting and disseminating papers and data sets. Digital preservation should be the core of the repository's purpose, but the work of digital preservation is much more involved than simply depositing resources. Preservation work includes ensuring secure backups, using fixity tools to detect any errors in digital files introduced over time, and employing strategies like migration and emulation to ensure the continued accessibility of digital files. Institutional repository software alone often has only limited preservation features and must be supplemented by external systems.

In the first few years of this century, many institutions established repositories and waited for the resources to pour in. They quickly realized, though, that recruiting content is one of the greatest challenges of running an institutional repository. A recent survey conducted by Li and Banach reveals that repository staff, not faculty, are still responsible for depositing much of the content in institutional repositories.[18] For many libraries, staff recruitment and deposit of materials inadvertently became part of their data services program. There are benefits to this: faculty do not always deposit materials that meet quality standards, and metadata is often better crafted by librarians than researchers. But the additional staffing this requires cannot be discounted.

Giesecke argues that institutional repositories run by a library are more likely to succeed when librarians see their roles more as publishers rather than collectors.[19] This mindset can lead to stronger collection development policies and a more cohesive, robust repository; it can also help the library uncover unexpected resources and opportunities. For example, Giesecke describes a reference work that had been compiled by researchers at the University of Nebraska, Lincoln, that had never found a suitable publisher. The repository coordinator found the work, a dictionary of invertebrate zoology, while working with a researcher, crafted it into an online document for repository deposit, and eventually began creating a print-on-demand version. The dictionary became a popular resource, and both the researcher and the library benefited. These kinds of projects can be excellent ways for libraries to participate in new ways in the scholarly communication ecosystem.

Institutional repositories can be a strong cornerstone of a library's data services program, but the implementation should not be taken lightly. Establishing an institutional repository is a long-term commitment to ensuring preservation and access to an institution's intellectual contributions. Institutional repositories require strong relationships between librarians and researchers and a solid sense of trust. The software itself may be free, but the ongoing management of a repository certainly is not.

If you are thinking of establishing an institutional repository, there are excellent resources available to help you in your planning and implementation process. Appendix A provides information about many of these resources.

IF A RESEARCHER DOES NOT WANT TO SUBMIT

In some instances, researchers are not willing to submit their data to an external repository. The data may be sensitive, or the researchers may not be ready to submit data or see the value of a particular data set being publicly available. In these instances, the researchers likely still need or want to make data available on a request basis. In such instances, talk to them not only about the preservation issues raised in chapter 6 but about how to provide even limited access to their data.

Some researchers are willing to have the metadata alone harvested and made available in discovery systems. You may choose to add institutional data set metadata to your local catalog or discovery system. You may want them to submit metadata only to a local repository, or to publish metadata on a website using a format that enables metadata harvesting, such the Open Archives Initiative Protocol for Metadata Harvesting (OAI-PMH, www.openarchives.org/pmh/). These techniques allow the information about a researcher's data to be made available, along with contact information so that those interested in learning more know how to get in touch with the researcher.

Some repositories do allow deposit without an open-access mandate. Encourage researchers to deposit in these repositories, if they are available, as a preservation precaution, even if they do not want their data to be widely available. Work with researchers to understand all the available licensing options. More information about these kinds of options is included in chapter 8. It should be possible to provide the benefits of preservation without the requirement of open access.

Helping researchers understand the difference between preservation and access, and walking through different access options with them, can help them understand these complex issues and make more informed choices about their own research data.

NOTES

1. See, for example, New York University's "Retention of and Access to Research Data," March 2010, www.nyu.edu/about/policies-guidelines-compliance/policies-and -guidelines/retention-of-and-access-to-research-data.html.
2. See Dryad's "Joint Data Archiving Policy," http://datadryad.org/pages/jdap.

3. University of Edinburgh, "Research Data Management Policy," June 2013, www .ed.ac.uk/schools-departments/information-services/about/policies-and-regulations/ research-data-policy; Ohio State University, "Policy on Institutional Data," October 2007, http://ocio.osu.edu/policy/policies/policy-on-institutional-data/; Stanford University, "Retention of and Access to Research Data," http://rph.stanford.edu/2-10.html.

4. "DMPTool," California Digital Library, July 2013, www.cdlib.org/services/uc3/dmp/ identifying.html.

5. "UC Curation Center: Curation Wiki," California Digital Library, July 2013, www .cdlib.org/services/uc3/curation/ark.html.

6. See the International DOI Foundation's DOI system website at www.doi.org.

7. Access the International Telecommunication Union's UUID procedures at www.itu .int/rec/T-REC-X.667-200409-S/en.

8. Access the International Union of Pure and Applied Chemistry's chemical identifier at http://iupac.org/home/publications/e-resources/inchi.html.

9. For more information on LSIDs, see http://en.wikipedia.org/wiki/LSID.

10. "Accession Number Prefixes: Where Are the Sequences From?" National Center for Biotechnology Information on GenBank accession numbers, www.ncbi.nlm.nih.gov/ Sequin/acc.html.

11. A. Whyte and G. Pryor, "Open Science in Practice: Researcher Perspectives and Participation," *International Journal of Digital Curation* 6, no. 1 (2011): 199–213.

12. V. B. Chaudhary, L. Walters, J. Bever, J. Hoeksema, and G. Wilson, "Advancing Synthetic Ecology: A Database System to Facilitate Complex Ecological Meta-Analyses," *Bulletin of the Ecological Society of America* 91, no. 2 (2010): 235–243.

13. K. Louis, L. Jones, and E. Campbell, "Sharing in Science," *American Scientist* 90, no. 4 (2002): 304–307.

14. H. Piwowar, R. Day, and D. Fridsma, "Sharing Detailed Research Data Is Associated with Increased Citation Rate," *PLoS ONE* 2, no. 3 (2007): e308. doi: 10.1371/journal .pone.0000308.

15. University of Southampton Library, "Restricting Access to Research Data," www .southampton.ac.uk/library/research/researchdata/restrictingaccess.html.

16. Access the Creative Commons (CC-0) license Zero via http://creativecommons.org/ publicdomain/zero/1.0/.

17. See Joan Giesecke, "Institutional Repositories: Keys to Success," *Journal of Library Administration* 51, no. 5/6 (2011): 529–542. doi:dx.doi.org/10.1080/01930826.2011 .589340.

18. Yuan Li and Meghan Banach, "Institutional Repositories and Digital Preservation: Assessing Current Practices at Research Libraries," *D-Lib Magazine* 17, no. 5/6 (2011). doi:10.1045/may2011-yuanli.

19. Giesecke, "Institutional Repositories."

Data Governance Issues

Among the most challenging issues related to data sharing is data governance.[1] Data governance is the system of rights, rules, and responsibilities that specify who can do what with data. This becomes complex for many reasons, mostly related to the number of stakeholders, institutions, and governing bodies involved. Despite the complexity, understanding the various laws and policies associated with data, and helping researchers unpack these, is critical to sharing data successfully.

Many of the skills needed to deal with data governance are those librarians already possess: experience dealing with licensing terms and agreements, knowledge about copyright, and the ability to read contracts carefully to suss out ownership issues.

WHY DATA GOVERNANCE?

One of the founding principles of scientific research is reproducibility; without data sharing, reproducibility is nearly impossible. Researchers who produce data and are unaware of the laws and regulations by which they should abide are less likely to share data for fear of legal action. To complicate the problem, providing a legal framework to ensure that data is openly available to everyone is not straightforward. To ensure reproducibility in research, we must enable data sharing; this requires careful consideration of the data governance framework.

The reusability of research is another critical component driving conversations about data governance. If policies are in place to ensure there are no barriers to using the data, then large-scale meta-analysis and the combination of disparate data sets from many laboratories, institutions, and countries become much more feasible. Without policies, uncertainties around data use can prevent or delay useful collaborations.

Data governance also becomes critical as more and more funders are requiring data management plans. A solid data management plan includes information about the policies associated with the data being produced. Per the National Science Foundation's grant proposal guidelines, the required data management plan supplement "may include . . . policies for access and sharing including provisions for appropriate protection of privacy, confidentiality, security, intellectual property, or other rights or requirements; [and] policies and provisions for re-use, re-distribution, and the production of derivatives."[2] Many researchers are unsure how to address these statements in their data management plans, partly through confusion about their institutions' policies and partly because of fear over lost rights or benefits from their data.

Researchers' fear of lost rights and benefits is easily addressed by a good understanding of data governance and a clear definition of the policies and procedures that others interested in using the data should follow. Researchers can, in fact, use solid knowledge of data governance to ensure that they get credit for all of their data by enacting clear licenses and rules for their work.

STAKEHOLDERS

Much of the complexity of data governance is related to the array of stakeholders in the data being produced. Various stakeholders have different needs from and investments in the data and are not always clear about their rights and responsibilities in relation to that data. Being aware of these issues when working with researchers can enable you to begin conversations with them about the relevant stakeholders in their own research and to consider the variety of concerns they might have and the issues that might apply.

Researchers are the first and clearest stakeholders. They often consider themselves "owners" of the data. Thus, they are often resistant to sharing and unwilling to place their data in a repository. This belief in data ownership stems from the confusion surrounding data policies and procedures and the fact that, until recently, most researchers had no need to share, explain, or provide access to their data sets.

A second stakeholder is the researcher's institution (and, by extension, institutional libraries). Researchers do not perform their research in a vacuum; their host institutions provide infrastructure and support that make data collection possible. Many institutions have standard forms related to patents and copyright that researchers are required to sign before starting work. Too often, however, this signing takes place without a thorough review of the policies, and with little guidance as to what is best for researchers or the data they will produce. As a librarian in your institution, you may be in a position to work with the departments responsible for these policies to ensure that they can accommodate the research data being produced in the institution and that they enable appropriate data sharing. You should try to initiate conversations with administrators and other institutional stakeholders about rights and responsibilities around the data produced at the institution.

Another stakeholder is the funder. Like the institution, funders provide resources that enable data collection and therefore are potentially able to lay claim to any data produced by their funds. They may also have forms or policies that the researcher must agree to, with little or no chance for consultation as to whether the forms are appropriate for their work. You might want to consult with researchers regarding funder policies to help them understand any requirements and policy implications regarding data ownership.

The wider academic publishing community is another stakeholding group. Publishers have a vested interest in ensuring that data supporting their publications is available to ensure reputability of the journal. In recent years many journals have begun enacting data-sharing requirements, which require researchers to make any data underlying their publication available. Researchers and librarians should be aware of the data requirements of journals in which they publish.

The final stakeholder in data governance is the public at large. Most research conducted at academic institutions is funded by taxpayer dollars via federal granting agencies such as the National Institutes of Health and the NSF. Sharing research data with accompanying clear policies for its use ensures that there is maximum gain from the data produced. It also helps eliminate redundant data collection, and the promotion of reproducibility helps reduce the reporting of unreliable results.

73

CURRENT STATUS OF DATA GOVERNANCE

Data and Copyright

Copyright is a form of protection for authors of "original works of authorship."[3] It is intended to protect the intellectual works of individuals, whether the work is published or unpublished. Only the copyright holder is able to reproduce the works, prepare derivatives, or distribute copies. Other rights include the right to be attributed as an author and the right to object to false attribution. The U.S. 1976 Copyright Act was enacted before digital data became a major currency in research and academia; it is therefore not written in a way that makes clear its application to data sets.

Part of the confusion surrounding data and copyright is that copyright does not apply to facts. Scientific data is, in most cases, an assimilation of facts. Importantly, however, copyright law distinguishes between facts and a collection of facts. This implies that data sets, databases, and other assimilations of data can be protected under copyright law. This may seem prohibitive to researchers' ability to build on the works of others, but researchers can use individual facts (i.e., data) from these assimilations without infringing on the original author's copyright.

The general rule of copyright ownership is that the creator of the material is the first owner, and that copyright can pass to another person only via written agreement.[4] This suggests that researchers are the owners of their data sets' copyright, but it is not always this simple. Often copyright may belong to the researcher's home institution or employer; in these cases, works produced in the course of normal employment are considered the employer's works. Check into your institution's policies to determine whether researchers own copyright to data sets produced while employed, and make sure that researchers are aware of these policies and any possible restrictions. Other stakeholders should also be considered; funders may require researchers to sign over copyright as a condition for funding.

Other Rights to Data

Another set of rights that may apply to data sets are known as sui generis (Latin, "unique in its characteristics") rights. Sui generis rights are intellectual property rights that prohibit the extraction or reuse of a database, regardless of creativity or originality of the database. Copyright law emphasizes creativity and originality; sui generis rights do not make this distinction. The European Union recognizes sui generis rights for fifteen years after database creation; the United States has not enacted such a law.[5] It may be worth while to pay attention to this topic in intellectual property law in the coming years.

Legal Mechanisms for Data Usage Rights

Copyright is automatic; no registration is required, and the owners automatically receive all rights to their work without any effort on their parts. For copyright owners to allow others access to their data sets, they must manage the copyright so that it permits others to use the data. This can be done using one of three legal mechanisms: licenses, contracts, or waivers. Choosing not to use any of these three mechanisms results in all rights for the data being reserved for the data owner, which inhibits data use and reuse.

Contracts for data use are also called access policies, data use policies, and data use licenses. The major benefit of contracts is that they are completely customizable; the copyright holder can dictate exactly who can have access and what those individuals can do with the data. Contracts can be problematic, however. Because they are customizable, they are more difficult to interpret and understand than a general or generic license. Often data use policies are created as "click-through agreements," wherein the person agreeing to the terms of the contract is unlikely to read it thoroughly, and therefore the contract may have limited enforceability. Contracts are also limited in their reach. If a user modifies the data slightly, with permission via a contract, then that data is now subject to the new user's contract agreements and copyright. In general, contracts have the potential to limit data use and reuse since the terms are often convoluted and difficult to understand, which discourages potential users who want to avoid legal retribution for data use.

Licenses are essentially a standardized form of a contract. The terms that apply for a given license are the same for any data released under that license. Data under license is therefore more usable and appealing to potential users, since there is less confusion about rights and responsibilities. Licenses are also more expansive in their reach than contracts; they apply to anyone who uses the data, regardless of where they find the material (e.g., if the data is posted on a second website by a colleague).

The use of licenses for data also has a fair number of risks. Copyright law is complicated, and most people who are creating and using licenses are not trained as copyright lawyers. As a result, the ad-hoc licenses they create may over- or underreach addressing copyrights associated with their dataset. Additionally, licenses are inflexible and therefore have the potential to discourage data use. For example, if a researcher is compiling data from multiple sources or databases, the licenses for each of those data sets must be considered, resulting in the potential for "attribution stacking." Attribution stacking occurs when it becomes infeasible to follow the terms of data licenses for all datasets used because it would result in an excessive number of authors, references, or other attributions.

The most commonly used licenses for digital content are those provided by Creative Commons (www.creativecommons.org). They consider four basic terms: attribution, derivation of works, noncommercial use, and sharing. The licenses offered by Creative Commons vary in these four terms, resulting in different licenses that clearly designate the rights of data users.

Waivers are a third legal mechanism for handling copyright of data. Waivers essentially place the data in the public domain; there are no legal restrictions to use by anyone. The Creative Commons Zero (CC-0) license is the most commonly used waiver; it waives all copyrights and allows unrestricted access to and use of the data. Waivers are beneficial in that they provide a legal certainty that users need not be concerned with potential rights infringement if the data is used. Waivers also eliminate the potential for interoperability problems when using multiple data sets, including preventing attribution stacking. The potential risk of using a waiver is that there is no legal recourse for the user failing to give credit to the original author. There is, however, a moral obligation to attribute original data creators for their work in the same way that research papers used to write a manuscript are attributed in the notes or bibliography.

PRIVACY AND CONFIDENTIALITY ISSUES

Data governance also encompasses considerations for privacy, confidentiality, and ethical issues that potentially compound the legal issues. There are laws associated with certain types of data, including those involving human subjects, endangered species, or indigenous lands. These laws may restrict researchers' abilities to share their data sets, regardless of copyright. As a result, tension exists between privacy and the current move toward open data, open science, and open research. It is important to note that licenses and waivers cannot address privacy and confidentiality; contracts must be used in cases where these types of issues may be important.

Institutional review boards exist to approve institutional research that is related to human subjects. The goal of such approval is to monitor and review research involving humans in order to protect them from harm, including release of personal data. The review board should be consulted for institution-specific information related to human subjects data. The HIPAA (Health Insurance Portability and Accountability Act of 1996) Privacy Rule provides federal protections for personal health information held by organizations such as hospitals and clinics; data under HIPAA protection is subject to special data governance considerations.

Many ethical questions can arise with regard to open access to data about endangered species or indigenous peoples and lands. Bernadette Callery writes, "The primary argument for limiting access to detailed locality data is the protection of economically exploitable objects from over-collecting."[6] When the locations of newly discovered or endangered species are published openly, that data is available not just to researchers in the field but to poachers and animal traders who exploit populations and contribute to the continued degradation of species.

The ethical and intellectual property issues related to field studies of indigenous communities, too, are complex. Knowledge gained from members of indigenous communities can be misappropriated. Members of these communities have the right to determine whether their knowledge is part of the public domain, and intellectual property issues should be negotiated with these communities. Additionally, research on these communities can lead to unintended outcomes in government policies and local economies.[7] Decisions about the openness of this kind of information cannot be made without the informed consent of the communities from which it is derived.

Many researchers working in fields involving endangered species, indigenous communities, or disciplines with human subjects are actively engaged in the process of negotiating new licenses and new frameworks for making available their research in respectful and safe ways. If you work with researchers who work in these fields, it can be helpful to ask what they know about these issues and how they might handle sensitive data.

FUTURE DIRECTIONS

The current status of data governance is murky at best; there is confusion about data ownership, stakeholder policies, rights to the use and reuse of data, and legal obligations related to data sets. The relative newness of digital data made widely available on the Internet makes these governance issues challenging. International collaborations are the norm in scientific research; any governance issues are compounded when multiple institutions in multiple countries are involved.

77

To address these challenges, many have called for a unified, community-driven body to collate existing policies and generate new standards for data governance. One such example is the call for a Data Governance Interoperability Panel, which was among the major outcomes of a data governance workshop hosted by Creative Commons and DataONE (an NSF-funded DataNet initiative) in December 2011. This panel would be challenged with such activities as clarifying current policies, determining criteria for data ownership, providing templates for data usage license agreements, and developing educational materials for stakeholders in the data governance arena.

The movement toward openness in science is evident in the rise of open-access journals, the push for mandated data sharing, and the increase in publicly available lab notebooks and databases. This openness is being met with resistance by some researchers who believe that their intellectual property is at risk by making their science open. Careful consideration of data governance and the use of licenses, waivers, and contracts has the potential to reduce the barriers to data sharing for these individuals. Moving forward with a broad set of publicly available, free, and agreed-upon licenses that address researchers' concerns about their intellectual property will make data sharing much more feasible in the future. Read more about open science and open data in chapter 7.

NOTES

1. Much of this chapter was informed by a data governance workshop sponsored by DataONE and Creative Commons, December 14–15, 2011, Washington, DC. In attendance were M. Smith, P. Cruse, C. Strasser, W. Michener, L. Dirks, R. Cook, M. Altman, G. Henry, J. Wilbanks, J. Kirchner, R. Koskela, A. Riley, S. Pearson, J. Rees, J. Greenberg, C. Greer, G. Grenier, R. Huffine, C. Lynch, D. Mietchen, A. Riley, A. Rizk-Jackson, R. Wilson, K. Ashley, R. Chadduck, C. Biemesderfer. More information is available at http://wiki.creativecommons.org/Data_governance _workshop.

2. Grant Proposal Guide, "Chapter II: Proposal Preparation Instructions," National Science Foundation, January 2011, www.nsf.gov/pubs/policydocs/pappguide/ nsf11001/gpg_2.jsp#IIC2gvib.

3. "Copyright Basics," United States Copyright Office, www.copyright.gov/circs/circ01 .pdf.

4. "Copyright and Data," Australian National Data Service, November 2009, http://ands .org.au/guides/copyright-and-data-awareness.html.

5. For an example of how these rights are handled, see "Sui Generis Right Protection," European Space Agency, www.esa.int/SPECIALS/Intellectual_Property_Rights/SEM3N2M26WD_0.html.

6. Bernadette G. Callery, "Patterns of Identification of Potentially Sensitive Data in Natural History Museum Online Catalogs," *Journal of Internet Cataloging* 7, no. 1 (January 2004): 103–115, 106 (quote).

7. Eric C. Kansa, Jason Schultz, and Ahrash N. Bissell, "Protecting Traditional Knowledge and Expanding Access to Scientific Data: Juxtaposing Intellectual Property Agendas via a Model," *International Journal of Cultural Property* 12, no. 3 (2005): 285–314. doi:10.1017/S0940739105050204.

Afterword

Data management is a big and complex issue, and there are many components that we do not cover in full here. Nevertheless, we hope this guide provides a good overview and an idea about how to start building data services in your library.

Scholarly communication has been undergoing rapid changes, and data is being included in this realm in ways it hasn't been before, thanks to the technologies that are now available. As this landscape changes, we librarians will struggle to find our place in it. It is important that we begin to take steps into this new world, even if we stumble while we try to find stable ground. Preservation and provision of access to scholarly information have always been the foundation of our mission as academic librarians, and as the form of scholarly information changes so must our practices, our infrastructures, and our organizations.

This can be an overwhelming new area, but there are many ways to step into it, depending on your resources and abilities. As long as you are collaborating with other stakeholders and key players in your institution, you will be able to craft the right services for your community. This is not something librarians can figure out on our own.

This is an exciting time for libraries, researchers, and even publishers. We can work now to define a better system for creating new knowledge, one that is accessible to more people and continues to make information available now and long into the future.

Resources for Institutional Repositories

For many libraries, establishing an institutional repository is the cornerstone of their data management service. There are many considerations to establishing a repository and ensuring its success. The following resources can help you think through your options, plan an implementation project, and build your repository with the support of your institution and faculty.

- Bailey, Charles W. *Institutional Repository Bibliography*. Houston, TX: Digital Scholarship, 2009. www.digital-scholarship.org/irb/irb.html.
- Barton, Mary R., and Margaret M. Waters. *Creating an Institutional Repository LEADIRS Workbook*. Cambridge: MIT Libraries, 2004. http://dspace.mit.edu/handle/1721.1/26698.
- Gibbons, Susan. *Establishing an Institutional Repository*. Chicago: ALA TechSource, 2004.
- Nabe, Jonathan. *Starting, Strengthening, and Managing Institutional Repositories: A How-to-Do-It Manual*. New York: Neal-Schuman, 2009.
- Swan, Alma, and Leslie Chan. "Establishing a Repository." Open Access Scholarly Information Sourcebook, 2009. www.openoasis.org/index.php?option=com_content&view=article&id=161&Itemid=354.

Sample Data Librarian Job Descriptions

Sample job descriptions from "Information Specialists and Data Librarians," Australian National Data Service, 2011, www.ands.org.au/guides/dmframework/ dmskills-information.html, originally published under a Creative Commons Attribution License.

Job Title: Data Librarian (HEW Level 6)

Job Purpose

The Data Librarian position is responsible for investigating and assisting with implementation of Library support services relating to description, storage and sharing of research metadata and datasets.

Main Duties

- Analyse information requirements relating to research data management by academics and assist with documentation of system specifications to meet these needs.
- Liaise extensively with research and Library staff to identify and collect information about data collections at the University.
- Assist with administration, analysis and reporting on Library study of academic research data management practices at the University.
- Develop, package, test and evaluate training resources for academic and Library staff to support standards-based research data management practices at the University.
- Investigate, document and assist with development of a register of metadata schemas for research dataset management.

- Create and edit metadata records for data collections to meet quality standards defined by the Australian National Data Service (ANDS).
- Assist with development, testing and documentation of services for registering and storing research metadata and datasets.
- Cooperate with all health and safety policies and procedures of the University and take all reasonable care that their actions or omissions do not impact on the health and safety of others in the University.
- Other duties as required, appropriate to the level of the position.

Principal Accountabilities

- Information about existing data collections and requirements relating to research data management by academics is documented and accessible.
- Data management training resources for academic and Library staff are delivered and evaluated.
- A register of metadata schemas for describing and managing research data is accessible by the University community.
- Support development of systems and services related to research data management.
- Work is carried out in ways that safeguard the OHS of staff and visitors, including contractors.

Environment

There is an emerging role for libraries to support, more directly, the research of their institutions and to improve the integration of library resources with practices of researchers throughout the research lifecycle—to incorporate the process as well as the outputs of an institution's research. Increasingly governments and funding bodies are requiring that research funded by them should be accessible beyond the life of the project. Well managed research data is fundamental for discovery of and access to research resources.

The Library provides a range of services to assist academic staff and postgraduate researchers to manage research resources. This includes research data and dataset management, development and support services for sharing information assets, and the management of scholarly outputs through an institutional repository. The Library participates in e-research projects and services supporting research data management needs of the University.

Selection Criteria

1. Extensive experience working with scholarly communication or research processes, through postgraduate qualifications and/or extensive relevant experience.
2. Demonstrated experience in the planning, implementation and reporting of information, research or data management projects or services.
3. Sound understanding of requirements for information management throughout the research lifecycle, including scholarly communication in a university or research environment.
4. Demonstrated experience in information management or content management, with knowledge of current technologies and standards such as institutional repositories, encoding standards (e.g. XML) and metadata.
5. Experience in developing and delivering training or support materials and services, including online products, in information management or a related area.
6. Demonstrated strong liaison, interpersonal, and communication skills, including the ability to build relationships across a range of professional and disciplinary areas
7. Demonstrated ability to work independently and with initiative, set priorities and balance the demands of a complex working environment.
8. Knowledge of OHS responsibilities and commitment to attending relevant OHS training.
9. Knowledge of equal opportunity principles.

Research Support Librarian

Fraction: Full time
Reports to: Associate Director, Library Services (Information Resources and Research Support)

Duty Statement

PURPOSE OF THE POSITION

The Research Support Librarian position provides leadership, service development, expertise and support for a range of research support activities including bibliometric and citation reporting, research data management and scholarly publishing strategies. The position provides strategic support to the development of new policies, procedures, resources and infrastructure for new research support services.

The position also provides these services to researchers and higher degree research students across all Faculties and Institutes of the University.

ORGANISATIONAL STRUCTURE AND RELATIONSHIPS
The position is located within the Library's Research Support Team, and works closely with Library Resource Services, Library eServices, the Branch Libraries, and the High Performance Computing and Research Support Team (within Information Technology Services) to coordinate and provide these services.

Duties Include:

1. Provide strategic support for the development of policy, procedures and templates for a regular and systematic bibliometric citation reporting service. Provide this reporting service to Assistant Deans Research and Institute Directors and provide advice on their usage.
2. Provide strategic support for the development of policy, procedures, infrastructure and resources for research data management services. Collaborate with High Performance Computing Services to provide this service, including promotion and training, to researchers and higher degree research students.
3. Provide strategic support for the development of policy, procedures and resources for publication strategy services. Provide this service to researchers and higher degree research students, including promotion, the selection of journals and conferences for publication, rankings, and open access publishing.
4. Provide strategic support for the development of policy, procedures and resources for general information management support services. Provide this service to researchers and higher degree research students, including advice on the selection and use of collaboration, workflow and content management software tools.
5. Scope, develop and provide integrated literacy and research skills development programs in blended mode, including training and online resources.
6. Work collaboratively with Associate Director, Library Services (Information Resources and Research Support), the Library's Research Support Team, Liaison Librarians, other Library staff, and High Performance Computing and Research Support staff to develop, provide and promote integrated research support services.
7. Deputise to the eResearch Access Coordinator (Team Leader) as required.

Selection Criteria

ESSENTIAL

1. Education, training and or experience equivalent to a postgraduate qualification in Library Science or Information Management in conjunction with significant relevant experience.
2. A well developed understanding of bibliometrics and citation analysis.
3. A well developed understanding of publishing strategies, rankings and open access.
4. A well developed understanding of research data management principles, practices and systems.
5. A well developed understanding of information management issues and solutions.
6. Demonstrated ability to scope and provided strategic support to the development of new services including policy, procedures, resources and infrastructure.
7. Demonstrated high level interpersonal, communication and facilitation skills, with the ability to liaise confidently with a large and diverse range of clients.
8. Demonstrated high level training delivery and people-centred skills, to enable the transfer of knowledge through training and development activities.
9. Proven ability to work as a member of multiple teams simultaneously.

DESIRABLE

1. Experience working in a scientific, technical or academic organisation.

Sample Data Management Plans

These sample data management plans are from the DataOne website: www.dataone .org/data-management-planning.

Example Data Management Plan

Background

Project name: Effects of temperature and salinity on population growth of the estuarine copepod, Eurytemora affinis

Description of project aims and purpose: We will rear populations of *E. affinis* in the laboratory at three temperatures and three salinities (9 treatments total). We will document the population from hatching to death, noting the proportion of individuals in each stage over time. The data collected will be used to parameterize population models of *E. affinis*. We will build a model of population growth as a function of temperature and salinity. This will be useful for studies of invasive copepod populations in the Northeast Pacific.

1. INFORMATION ABOUT DATA

Every two days, we will subsample *E. affinis* populations growing at our treatment conditions. We will use a microscope to identify the stage and sex of the subsampled individuals. We will document the information first in a laboratory notebook, then copy the data into an Excel spreadsheet. For quality control, values will be entered separately by two different people to ensure accuracy. The Excel spreadsheet will be saved as a comma-separated value (.csv) file daily and backed up to a server. After all data are collected, the Excel spreadsheet will be saved as a .csv file and imported into the program R for statistical analysis. Strasser will be responsible for all data management during and after data collection.

Our short-term data storage plan, which will be used during the experiment, will be to save copies of 1) the .txt metadata file and 2) the Excel spreadsheet as .csv files to an external drive, and to take the external drive off site nightly. We will use the Subversion version control system to update our data and metadata files daily on the University of Alberta Mathematics Department server. We will also have the laboratory notebook as a hard copy backup.

2. METADATA FORMAT AND CONTENT

We will first document our metadata by taking careful notes in the laboratory notebook that refer to specific data files and describe all columns, units, abbreviations, and missing value identifiers. These notes will be transcribed into a .txt document that will be stored with the data file. After all of the data are collected, we will then use EML (Ecological Metadata Language) to digitize our metadata. EML is one of the accepted formats used in Ecology, and works well for the type of data we will be producing. We will create these metadata using Morpho software, available through the Knowledge Network for Biocomplexity (KNB). The documentation and metadata will describe the data files and the context of the measurements.

3. POLICIES FOR ACCESS, SHARING, AND REUSE

We are required to share our data with the CAISN network. After all data have been collected and metadata have been generated. This should be no more than 6 months after the experiments are completed. In order to gain access to CAISN data, interested parties must contact the CAISN data manager (data@caisn.ca) or the authors and explain their intended use. Data requests will be approved by the authors after review of the proposed use.

The authors will retain rights to the data until the resulting publication is produced, within two years of data production. After publication (or after two years, whichever is first), the authors will open data to public use. After publication, we will submit our data to the KNB allowing discovery and use by the wider scientific community. Interested parties will be able to download the data directly from KNB without contacting the authors, but will still be required to give credit to the authors for the data used by citing a KNB accession number either in the publication's text or in the references list.

4. LONG-TERM STORAGE AND DATA MANAGEMENT (ARCHIVING)

The data set will be submitted to KNB for long-term preservation and storage. The authors will submit metadata in EML format along with the data to facilitate its reuse. Strasser will be responsible for updating metadata and data author contact information in the KNB.

Example Data Management Plan, based on the work of C. D. Keeling and Colleagues, Scripps Institution of Oceanography

Background

This example data management plan illustrates the key elements required for a two-page plan for an NSF proposal.

We have chosen to use an iconic data product—the Keeling Mauna Loa CO_2 record—for this example Data Management Plan. All environmental scientists are familiar with this data record. It is posted in the atrium of the U.S. National Academy of Sciences, next to the DNA Double helix. We are writing this Data Management Plan as if it were to be included in an NSF proposal in 2011.

Data Management Plan

1. INTRODUCTION AND CONTEXT

The purpose of this proposed project is to study the controls on the concentration of atmospheric CO_2 using high precision and accuracy measurements at a remote island observatory.

We propose to measure the concentrations of CO_2 in the atmosphere at the Mauna Loa Observatory, Hawaii. The methodology for sample collection and analysis during this proposed project will generate highly accurate and precise data that can be seamlessly added to the existing Mauna Loa CO_2 record (1958–2010) [1,2]. A major theme for this project is to identify and minimize systematic measurement errors through rigorous sampling and calibration procedures.

2. INFORMATION ABOUT THE DATA

Air samples at Mauna Loa Observatory will be collected continuously from air intakes located at five towers—a central tower and four towers located at compass quadrants. Raw data files will contain continuously measured CO_2 concentrations, calibration standards, references standards, daily check standards, and blanks. The sample lines located at compass quadrants were used to examine the influence of source effects associated with wind directions [3,4]. In addition to the CO_2 data, we will record weather data (wind speed and direction, temperature, humidity, precipitation, and cloud cover). Site conditions at Mauna Loa Observatory will also be noted and retained.

The final data product will consist of 5-minute, 15-minute, hourly, daily, and monthly average atmospheric concentration of CO_2, in mole fraction in water-vapor-free air measured at the Mauna Loa Observatory, Hawaii. Data are reported as a dry mole fraction defined as the number of molecules of CO_2 divided by the number of molecules of dry air multiplied by one million (ppm).

The final data product has been thoroughly documented in the open literature [2] and in Scripps Institution of Oceanography Internal Reports [1]. The data generated (raw CO_2 measurements, meteorological data, calibration and reference standards) will be placed in comma-separated-values in plain ASCII format, which are readable over long time periods. The final data file will contain dates for each observation (time, day, month and year) and the average CO_2 concentration. The final data product distributed to most users will occupy less than 500 KB; raw and ancillary data, which will be distributed on request, will occupy less than 10 MB.

3. METADATA CONTENT AND FORMAT

Metadata will be comprised of two formats—contextual information about the data in a text based document and ISO 19115 standard metadata in an xml file. These two formats for metadata were chosen to provide a full explanation of the data (text format) and to ensure compatibility with international standards (xml format). The standard XML file will be more complete; the document file will be a human-readable summary of the XML file.

4. SHORT-TERM STORAGE AND DATA MANAGEMENT

The data product will be updated monthly due to updates to the record, revisions due to recalibration of standard gases, and due to errors. The date of the update will be included in the data file and will be part of the data file name. Versions of the data product that have been revised due to errors / updates (other than new data) will be retained in an archive system. A revision history document will describe the revisions made.

Daily and monthly backups of the data files will be retained at the Keeling Group Lab (http://scrippsco2.ucsd.edu , accessed 05/2011), at the Scripps Institution of Oceanography Computer Center, and at the Woods Hole Oceanographic Institution's Computer Center.

5. POLICIES FOR ACCESS AND SHARING

The final data product will be release to the public as soon as the recalibration of standard gasses has been completed and the data have been prepared, typically within six months of collection. There is no period of exclusive use by the data collectors. Users can access documentation and final monthly CO_2 data files via the Scripps CO_2 Program website (http://scrippsco2.ucsd.edu). The data will be made available via ftp download from the Scripps Institution of Oceanography Computer Center. Raw data (continuous concentration measurements, weather data, etc.) will be maintained on an internally accessible server and made available on request at no charge to the user.

6. LONG-TERM STORAGE AND DATA MANAGEMENT (ARCHIVING)

Our intent is that the long-term high quality final data product generated by this project will be available for use by the research and policy communities in perpetuity. The raw supporting data will be available in perpetuity as well, for use by researchers to confirm the quality of the Mauna Loa Record. The investigators have made arrangements for long-term stewardship and curation at the Carbon Dioxide Information and Analysis Center (CDIAC), Oak Ridge National Laboratory (see letter of support). The standardized metadata record for the Mauna Loa CO_2 data will be added to the metadata record database at CDIAC, so that interested users can discover the Mauna Loa CO_2 record along with other related Earth science data. CDIAC has a standardize data product citation [5] including DOI, that indicates the version of the Mauna Loa Data Product and how to obtain a copy of that product.

REFERENCES
[would be located with other References in Proposal body]

[1] Keeling, CD, SC Piper, RB Bacastow, M Wahlen, TP Whorf, M Heimann, and HA Meijer, **2001.** Exchanges of atmospheric CO_2 and $^{13}CO_2$ with the terrestrial biosphere and oceans from 1978 to 2000. I. Global aspects, SIO Reference Series, No. 01-06, Scripps Institution of Oceanography, San Diego CA, 88 pages.

[2] Keeling, CD, SC Piper, RB Bacastow, M Wahlen, TP Whorf, M Heimann, and HA Meijer, **2005.** Atmospheric CO_2 and $^{13}CO_2$ exchange with the terrestrial biosphere and oceans from 1978 to 2000: observations and carbon cycle implications, In *A History of Atmospheric CO_2 and its effects on Plants, Animals, and Ecosystems.* Edited by JR Ehleringer, TE Cerling, and MD Dearing, Springer Verlag, New York, pages 83-113.

[3] Bacastow, RB, CD Keeling, and TP Whorf, **1985.** Seasonal amplitude increase in atmospheric CO_2 concentration at Mauna Loa, Hawaii, 1959-1982. J. Geophys. Res. 90, 10529-10540.

[4] Sundquist, ET and RF Keeling, **2009.** The Mauna Loa Carbon Dioxide Record: Lessons for Long-Earth Observations. In *Carbon Sequestration and Its Role in the*

Global Carbon Cycle. AGU Monograph Series 183. Edited by BJ McPherson and ET Sundquist. pages 27-35. doi: 10.1029/2008GM000713.

[5] Keeling, RF, SC Piper, AF Bollenbacher and JS Walker, **2009.** Atmospheric CO_2 records from sites in the SIO air sampling network. In *Trends: A Compendium of Data on Global Change*. Carbon Dioxide Information Analysis Center, Oak Ridge National Laboratory, Oak Ridge, TN, doi: 10.3334/CDIAC/atg.035.

About the Authors

Laura Krier

Laura Krier is a metadata librarian at the California Digital Library in Oakland, California. She works on projects ranging from data modeling and analysis to research into linked data models for libraries. She received an MS from Simmons Graduate School of Library and Information Science and a BA from the University of California–Santa Cruz.

Carly A. Strasser

Carly A. Strasser is a data curation specialist at the California Digital Library, University of California Office of the President. She has a PhD in biological oceanography, which informs her work on helping researchers better manage and share their data. She is involved in development and implementation of many of the UC Curation Center's services, including the DMPTool (software to guide researchers in creating a data management plan) and DataUp (an application that helps researchers organize, manage, and archive their tabular data).

Index